HOW TO TELL THE DIFFERENCE BETWEEN JAPANESE PARTICLES

HOW TO TELL THE DIFFERENCE BETWEEN JAPANESE PARTICLES

Comparisons and Exercises

Naoko Chino

KODANSHA INTERNATIONAL
Tokyo · New York · London

Distributed in the United States by Kodansha America, Inc., and in the United Kingdom and continental Europe by Kodansha Europe Ltd.

Published by Kodansha International Ltd., 17–14 Otowa 1-chome, Bunkyo-ku, Tokyo 112–8652, and Kodansha America, Inc.

Copyright © 2005 by Naoko Chino.
All rights reserved. Printed in Japan.
ISBN 978-4-7700-2200-4

First edition, 2005
15 14 13 12 11 10 09 08 07   10 9 8 7 6 5 4 3

www.kodansha-intl.com

CONTENTS

Preface 9

I   Particles Indicating Time   11

1. に (ni), 2. から (kara), 3. まで (made), 4. までに (made ni), 5. から…まで (kara … made), 6. より (yori), 7. ほど (hodo), 8. くらい、ぐらい (kurai, gurai), 9. ころ、ごろ (koro, goro), 10. ばかり (bakari)

QUIZ I —— 17

II   Particles that Indicate the Place Where an Action Takes Place or the Place Where Something Is (Exists)   23

1. で (de), 2a-b-c. に (ni), 3. の (no), 4. へ／に (e/ni)

QUIZ II —— 28

III   Particles Showing Connections between Words   31

1. と (to), 2. も (mo), 3. も…も (mo … mo), 4. や (ya), 5. や…や…など (ya … ya … nado), 6. に (ni), 7. とか (to ka), 8. やら (yara), 9. て (-te), 10a-b. たり…たり (-tari … -tari), 11. ては (-te wa)

QUIZ III —— 39

IV   Particles that Indicate Direction   45

1. に／へ (ni/e), 2. から (kara), 3. から…まで (kara … made), 4. より (yori)

QUIZ IV —— 48

V   Particles that Indicate a Question or Uncertainty   53

1a-b. か (ka), 2. かな (ka na), 3. かしら (kashira), 4. の (no), 5. って (tte)

QUIZ V —— 57

VI   Particles that Indicate a Reason or Cause   61

1. て (-te), 2. で (de), 3. から (kara), 4. ので (no de), 5. もので (mono de)

QUIZ VI —— 65

VII   Particles that Indicate a Condition or Supposition   71

1. ば (-ba), 2. たら (-tara), 3. なら (nara), 4. ところで (tokoro de), 5. ても、でも (-te mo, -de mo), 6. と (to)

QUIZ VII —— 75

VIII   Particles that Indicate a Limitation or Maximum   79

1. しか (shika), 2. だけ (dake), 3. だけしか (dake shika), 4. のみ (nomi), 5. きり (kiri), 6. きりしか (kiri shika), 7. のみしか (nomi shika)

QUIZ VIII —— 84

IX   Particles Indicating, or Providing Information about, the Subject of a Clause or Sentence   89

1a-c. は (wa), 2. が (ga), 3. で (de), 4. も (mo), 5. として (toshite), 6. には (ni wa)

QUIZ IX —— 97

X   Particles that Indicate Objects of Desire or Wishes   101

1. を (o), 2. が (ga), 3. に／へ (ni/e)

 —— 104

XI Particles that Indicate a List of Objects, Qualities, or Actions — 107

1. や…や (ya ... ya), 2. とか…とか (to ka ... to ka), 3. だの…だの (dano... dano), 4. など (nado), 5. なんか (nanka), 6. に (ni)

QUIZ XI —— 113

XII Particles that Indicate an Amount or Quantity — 117

1. くらい、ぐらい (kurai, gurai), 2. ほど (hodo), 3. ばかり、ばかし (bakari, bakashi), 4. ずつ (zutsu), 5. とも (tomo), 6. だけ (dake), 7. も (mo)

QUIZ XII —— 123

XIII The Particle の (No) Indicates that the Noun Preceding It Modifies the Noun Following It — 127

1. の (no)

QUIZ XIII —— 129

XIV Sentence-ending Particles Indicating What the Speaker Has Heard — 131

1. って (tte), 2. だと (da to)

QUIZ XIV —— 134

XV Particles that Indicate Emphasis — 139

1. も (mo), 2. こそ (koso), 3. さえ (sae), 4. すら (sura), 5. ものなら (mono nara), 6. くせに (kuse ni), 7. どころか (dokoro ka), 8. ものを (mono o), 9. ぞ (zo), 10. ってば (tteba), 11. ものか (mono ka), 12. ほど (hodo)

QUIZ XV —— 147

XVI Particles Used for Comparison — 151

1. と (to), 2. より (yori), 3. ほど (hodo), 4. で (de)

QUIZ XVI —— 155

XVII Particles that Indicate a Means by which Something Is Done or Material from which Something Is Made — 157

1. で (de), 2. で、から (de, kara)

QUIZ XVII —— 159

XVIII Particles that Indicate a Purpose or Object of a Verb — 161

1. に (ni), 2. を (o)

QUIZ XVIII —— 163

XIX Particles that Come at the End of a Sentence and Indicate the Speaker's Feelings or Dictate the Tone of a Sentence — 167

1. か (ka), 2. さ (sa), 3. じゃん (jan), 4. けど (kedo), 5. な、なあ (na, nā), 6. もの (mono), 7. の (no), 8. ね (ne), 9. や (ya), 10. よ (yo), 11. わ (wa), 12. やら (yara), 13. が (ga), 14. から、ので (kara, no de)

QUIZ XIX —— 177

General Quiz — 181

Index of Particles (Romanized) 197
Index of Particles (Hiragana) 198

PREFACE

Many students seem to believe that the particle represents one of the most difficult aspects of the Japanese language. However, I believe that if students study the functions of particles one at a time and do this with proper understanding, it is not as difficult as it might seem to grasp their proper usage. In 1991 I selected the particles needed at an elementary and intermediate level, provided commentary, and published the results as *All About Particles* (Kodansha International). In the present book I have taken a new approach to many of the same particles, categorizing them by similarity in function and providing quizzes. I have not covered all the particles and functions in *All About Particles,* but only those that can be usefully compared with other particles.

Features of this book. The principal feature of this book is the categorizing of particles by function. According to this method, it should be clearer why certain particles are used in certain situations. Instead of studying similar particles independently and without reference to one another, students can now see particles with similar functions arranged together so that they can be easily compared.

The quizzes are also a main feature. One or more quizzes are placed at the end of each group of particles, so that students can immediately check and reinforce their understanding after finishing a particle group. There is also a General Quiz at the end of the book for review. For students preparing for the Japanese Language Proficiency Test, or other tests, these quizzes should provide good practice. The quizzes also serve a secondary purpose, filling the role traditionally played by textbook exercises.

Organization of this book. Many of the particles that invariably appear in beginning and intermediate Japanese studies have been categorized into nineteen groups by similarity of function. The number of particles varies from group to group. The order of the particles in a group follows the rule of the more frequent and easier particles coming first. Each group consists of the following parts:

1. Commentary on the function of each particle, with notes about specific differences where necessary; larger differences are often obvious from the general description of the particle.
2. Examples of the particles in full sentences.
3. Quizzes and the answers to the quizzes, as well as translations.

At the end of the book is the General Quiz section, which covers all the particles in the book. Each problem in this section is followed by the group number in which the relevant particle is discussed, for those who wish to refer back to the main text.

How to use this book. For those who are fairly confident of their understanding of particles, as well as for those who are preparing for the Japanese Language Proficiency Test, I suggest that you go immediately to the General Quiz and test your ability. If you find yourself making mistakes and are not sure of which answer is correct, you can follow the number at the end of the problem area and go to the main text to refresh your understanding. For less confident students who wish to approach the study of particles in a methodical manner, I recommend working your way through the book from beginning to end, tackling the General Quiz only after finishing the rest of the book.

In conclusion, I wish to express my hope that this book will prove itself useful. At the same time, I would like to thank Michael Brase, who provided the translations and made contributions to the commentary from his perspective as a longtime student of the language. My thanks also go out to Ayako Akaogi and others at Kodansha International for making the book possible.

Naoko Chino

I

Particles Indicating Time

1. に (ni)
2. から (kara)
3. まで (made)
4. までに (made ni)
5. から…まで (kara … made)
6. より (yori)
7. ほど (hodo)
8. くらい、ぐらい (kurai, gurai)
9. ころ、ごろ (koro, goro)
10. ばかり (bakari)

1. に (ni). Used after words indicating the specific point in time (e.g., "three o'clock") at which—or a interval (e.g., "one week") during which—an action takes place. English equivalent: "at."

i) 明日の会議は3時に始まります。
   Ashita no kaigi wa sanji **ni** hajimarimasu.
   Tomorrow's meeting will start at 3:00.

ii) 1週間に1回ピアノのレッスンに行きます。
   Isshūkan **ni** ikkai piano no ressun ni ikimasu.
   I go to have a piano lesson once a week.

✍ Some words that indicate time do not take に (ni). For example,

Days (日 **hi**)**:** yesterday (昨日 kinō), today (今日 kyō), tomorrow (明日 ashita)

Weeks (週 **shū**)**:** last week (先週 senshū), this week (今週 konshū), next week (来週 raishū)

Months (月 **tsuki**)**:** last month (先月 sengetsu), this month (今月 kongetsu), next month (来月 raigetsu)

i) 今週は寒い日が多い。
Konshū wa samui hi ga ōi.
There have been a lot of cold days this week.

ii) 来月海外旅行に行く。
Raigetsu kaigai-ryokō ni iku.
I'm going to make a trip abroad next month.

> 🖉 Some words indicating time can either take に (ni) or not take it. For example,
>
> **Seasons (季節 kisetsu):** spring (春 haru), summer (夏 natsu), fall (秋 aki), winter (冬 fuyu)

i) 冬は東京にいますが、夏にはハワイに行きます。
Fuyu wa Tōkyō ni imasu ga, **natsu ni** wa Hawai ni ikimasu.
I'll be in Tokyo in winter, but I will go to Hawaii in summer.

ii) 去年の秋は韓国にいました。
Kyonen no **aki** wa Kankoku ni imashita.
I was in Korea last fall.

2. から (kara). Indicates the point in time from which an action commences. から is sometimes interchangeable with に (ni; I-1), but even then it places more emphasis on the starting point (see third sample below, where から could be replaced by に). English equivalents: "from," "at."

i) 学校は8時半**から**です。
Gakkō wa hachiji-han **kara** desu.
School starts at 8:30.

ii) 投票ができるのは、20歳**から**です。
Tōhyō ga dekiru no wa, hatachi **kara** desu.
You can vote from the age of twenty.

iii) 明日の会議は3時**から**始まります。
Ashita no kaigi wa sanji **kara** hajimarimasu.
Tomorrow's meeting will start from 3:00.

3. まで (made). Indicates the time at which a continuous action comes to an end, or the moment at which something occurs (such as when one gets tired) that brings a continuous action to an end. English equivalents: "until."

i) 会議は3時半**まで**続きました。
Kaigi wa sanji-han **made** tsuzukimashita.
The meeting continued until 3:30.

ii) 昨日は遅く**まで**仕事をした。
Kinō wa osoku **made** shigoto o shita.
Yesterday I worked until late.

iii) 疲れる**まで**走ろう。
Tsukareru **made** hashirō.
Let's run until we're tired out.

4. までに (made ni). Indicates the time by which something will or must be finished. までに is basically setting a time limit, whereas まで (made; I-3) is simply stating the fact that something continued from this point in time to that. The two are most easily distinguished by remembering their English equivalents. English equivalent: "by."

i) 明日10時**までに**、空港に集まってください。
Ashita jūji **made ni**, kūkō ni atsumatte kudasai.
Meet up at the airport by 10:00 tomorrow.

ii) この書類のコピーを昼**までに**取らなければなりません。
Kono shorui no kopī o hiru **made ni** toranakereba narimasen.
I have to make a copy of this document by noon.

5. から…まで (kara ... made). A combination of から (kara; I-2) and まで (made; I-3). Indicates the starting point and ending point of an interval of time during which an action takes place. English equivalent: "from ... to."

    i) 仕事は月曜日**から**金曜日**まで**です。
       Shigoto wa getsuyōbi **kara** kin'yōbi **made** desu.
       Work/my job is from Monday to Friday.

    ii) デパートは10時**から**8時**まで**開いています。
       Depāto wa jūji **kara** hachiji **made** aite imasu.
       The department store is open from 10:00 to 8:00.

6. より (yori). Like から (kara; I-2), indicates the point in time from which an action commences, but より has a more formal or official sound. English equivalent: "from."

    i) 大統領の記者会見は3時**より**行われる。
       Daitōryō no kisha-kaiken wa sanji **yori** okonawareru.
       The President's press conference will be held from 3:00.

    ii) 入社式は午前10時**より**11時半までの予定。
       Nyūsha-shiki wa gozen jūji **yori** jūichiji-han made no yotei.
       The ceremony to welcome new employees is scheduled to be held from 10:00 until 11:30 A.M.

7. ほど (hodo). Indicates an approximate amount of time, with the slight connotation that the figure given is the maximum. It has a formal ring to it. English equivalent: "approximately."

    i) 電車の到着は、事故のため30分**ほど**遅れます。
       Densha no tōchaku wa, jiko no tame sanjuppun **hodo** okuremasu.
       Due to an accident, the train will be approximately 30 minutes late.

ii) 今会社を出ますので、後15分**ほど**したらそちらに伺います。
Ima kaisha o demasu no de, ato jūgo-fun **hodo** shitara sochira ni ukagaimasu.
I am leaving the office now, so I will arrive there (where you are) in approximately 15 minutes.

8. くらい、ぐらい (kurai, gurai). Indicates an approximate amount of time, with the slight connotation that the figure given is the minimum. This particle does not have the formal sound of ほど (hodo; I-7). くらい and ぐらい are interchangeable. English equivalent: "about," "around."

i) 家から会社まで、40分**くらい**かかります。
Ie kara kaisha made, yonjuppun **kurai** kakarimasu.
It takes about 40 minutes from home to the office.

ii) 仕事が後5分**くらい**で終わりますので、少しお待ちください。
Shigoto ga ato gofun **kurai** de owarimasu no de, sukoshi omachi kudasai.
The work will be finished in another five minutes or so, so please wait a bit longer.

9. ころ、ごろ (koro, goro). Indicates approximation when referring to a point in time. The two particles are largely interchangeable. Compare this with に (ni; I-1), which indicates an exact point in time, and くらい、ぐらい (kurai, gurai; I-8) which indicate an approximate amout of time. English equivalents: "around," "about."

i) 3時**ごろ**、そちらに伺います。
Sanji **goro**, sochira ni ukagaimasu.
I will call on you around 3:00.

ii) 毎朝6時**ごろ**起きます。
Maiasa rokuji **goro** okimasu.
I get up every morning around 6:00.

10. ばかり (bakari). Follows a verb in the past tense and indicates that an action has just been concluded. English equivalent: "just."

i) 山岡：遅くなりました。お待たせして、すみません。
多田：いいえ、私も今来た**ばかり**です。
Yamaoka: Osoku narimashita. Omatase shite, sumimasen.
Tada: Iie, watashi mo ima kita **bakari** desu.

Yamaoka: I am sorry to be late and to keep you waiting.
Tada: Don't mention it. I have just arrived myself.

ii) 母：掃除した**ばかり**なのに、もう散らかしたのね。
息子：だって、おもちゃで遊びたいんだもの。
Haha: Sōji shita **bakari** na no ni, mō chirakashita no ne.
Musuko: Datte, omocha de asobitai n' da mono.

Mother: I just finished cleaning and here you are already making a mess.
Son: But, I want to play with my toys.

QUIZ I

QUIZ I–1

Fill in the blanks with the choices given below each sentence. X indicates that a particle is not required. Answers are at the end of the quiz, along with English translations.

1. 駅から会社まで、何分（　　）かかりますか？
   Eki kara kaisha made, nanpun (　　) kakarimasu ka?

   1. まで (made)　2. ぐらい (gurai)　3. から (kara)　4. より (yori)

2. 明日は朝7時（　　）空港へ行かなければなりません。
   Ashita wa asa shichiji (　　) kūkō e ikanakereba narimasen.

   1. までに (made ni)　2. ぐらい (gurai)　3. から (kara)　4. ほど (hodo)

3. 社長は午後2時から4時（　　）会議に出席されます。
   Shachō wa gogo niji kara yoji (　　) kaigi ni shusseki saremasu.

   1. ぐらい (gurai)　2. より (yori)　3. まで (made)　4. に (ni)

4. 花子：今週の土曜日、ひま？
   美子：土曜日は忙しいけど、日曜日（　　）はひまよ。
   Hanako: Konshū no doyōbi, hima?
   Yoshiko: Doyōbi wa isogashii kedo, nichiyōbi (　　) wa hima yo.

   1. まで (made)　2. くらい (kurai)　3. X　4. ほど (hodo)

5. 首相主催の夕食会は、6時（　　）の予定。
   Shushō-shusai no yūshoku-kai wa, rokuji (　　) no yotei.

   1. に (ni)　2. より (yori)　3. ほど (hodo)　4. くらい (kurai)

6. 息子は来月（　　）米国に留学します。
   Musuko wa raigetsu (　　) Beikoku ni ryūgaku shimasu.

   1. ほど (hodo)　2. に (ni)　3. X　4. くらい (kurai)

7. 後30分（　　）で仕事が終わります。
   Ato sanjuppun (　　) de shigoto ga owarimasu.

   1. に (ni)　2. ぐらい (gurai)　3. から (kara)　4. まで (made)

8. 武：昨日の夜10時（　　）電話したけど、でなかったね。
   緑：ごめん、もう寝てたの。
   Takeshi: Kinō no yoru jūji (　　) denwa shita kedo, denakatta ne.
   Midori: Gomen, mō nete 'ta no.

   1. ほど (hodo)　2. から (kara)　3. ごろ (goro)　4. まで (made)

9. 靖彦：明日の授業、何時から何時（　　）？
   安夫：明日は授業ないよ。
   Yasuhiko: Ashita no jugyō, nanji kara nanji (　　)?
   Yasuo: Ashita wa jugyō nai yo.

   1. に (ni)　2. ほど (hodo)　3. より (yori)　4. まで (made)

10. 毎朝7時から1時間（　　）ジョギングをしています。
    Maiasa shichiji kara ichiji-kan (　　) jogingu o shite imasu.

    1. まで (made)　2. ぐらい (gurai)　3. に (ni)　4. から (kara)

Answers and Translations for Quiz I-1

1 = 2. About how long (how many minutes) does it take from the station to the office?
2 = 1. I have to be at (go to) the airport by 7:00 tomorrow morning.
3 = 3. The President will be attending a meeting from 2:00 in the afternoon to 4:00.
4 = 3. Hanako: You free this Saturday? Yoshiko: I'm busy Saturday but free Sunday.
5 = 2. The dinner being hosted by the Prime Minister is scheduled to start at 6:00.
6 = 3. Next month my son will be going to the United States to study.
7 = 2. The work will be finished in another 30 minutes or so. / I'll be finished with work in another 30 minutes or so.
8 = 3. Takeshi: I called you about 10 o'clock last night, but you didn't answer. Midori: I'm sorry. I had already gone to bed.
9 = 4. Yasuhiko: How long (from what time to what time) is the class going to last tomorrow? Yasuo: There isn't any class tomorrow.
10 = 2. I go jogging for about an hour every morning from 7:00.

QUIZ I-2

Choose the correct particle from among those within the parentheses. X indicates that no particle is necessary. Answers and English translations are given at the end of the quiz.

1. アメリカ旅行に行ったんだってね。ニューヨークには何日(から｜ぐらい)何日(に｜まで)いたの？
   Amerika-ryokō ni itta n' datte ne. Nyūyōku ni wa nannichi (kara | gurai) nannichi (ni | made) ita no?

2. 昨日は疲れて、昼ご飯の後、一時間(ごろ｜ぐらい)昼寝をした。
   Kinō wa tsukarete, hiru-gohan no ato, ichiji-kan (goro | gurai) hirune o shita.

3. 来春(X｜まで)大学を卒業したら、銀行に就職したい。
   Raishun (X | made) daigaku o sotsugyō shitara, ginkō ni shūshoku shitai.

4. コンサートは何時（から｜に）ですか？
   Konsāto wa nanji (kara | ni) desu ka?

5. 仕事は何時（X｜に）始まりますか？
   Shigoto wa nanji (X | ni) hajimarimasu ka?

6. 海外出張の予定は来月（X｜ほど）ですか、今月（に｜X）ですか？
   Kaigai-shutchō no yotei wa raigetsu (X | hodo) desu ka, kongetsu (ni | X) desu ka?

7. 3時（より｜X）大臣の記者会見が予定されている。
   Sanji (yori | X) daijin no kisha-kaiken ga yotei sarete iru.

8. 明日の宴会は夜おそく（まで｜までに）かかりそうだ。
   Ashita no enkai wa yoru osoku (made | made ni) kakarisō da.

9. 来週の月曜日、朝10時（までに｜ほど）会社に来られますか？
   Raishū no getsuyōbi, asa jūji (made ni | hodo) kaisha ni koraremasu ka?

10. あのデパートは、毎日（X｜に）10時（に｜まで）開店する。
    Ano depāto wa, mainichi (X | ni) jūji (ni | made) kaiten suru.

Answers and Translations for Quiz I-2

1 = から (kara), まで (made). I hear you made a trip to America. How long (from what day to what day) were you in New York?
2 = ぐらい (gurai). I was so tired yesterday I took a nap for about an hour after lunch.
3 = X. Next spring, when I've graduated from college, I want to find work in a bank.
4 = から (kara). What time is the concert from?
5 = に (ni). What time does work start?
6 = X, X. Is your business trip abroad scheduled for next month or for this month?
7 = より (yori). The Minister's press conference is scheduled to start from three o'clock.
8 = まで (made). The party tomorrow looks like it will go on until late.
9 = までに (made ni). Next Monday morning, can you come to the office by 10:00?
10 = X, に (ni). That department store opens at 10:00 every day.

II

Particles that Indicate the Place Where an Action Takes Place or the Place Where Something Is (Exists)

1. で (de)
2a-b-c. に (ni)
3. の (no)
4. へ／に (e/ni)

1. で (de). Indicates the place where an action takes place. Compare this with に (ni; II-2c), which has a similar function with a limited number of verbs. English equivalent: "at," "in."

i) 毎日、朝食は家で食べます。
Mainichi, chōshoku wa ie **de** tabemasu.
I eat breakfast at home every day.

ii) 山田さんは、銀座のデパートで働いています。
Yamada-san wa, Ginza no depāto **de** hataraite imasu.
Yamada-san works at a department store in Ginza.

iii) 第1回目のオリンピックは、ギリシャで開かれました。
Daiikkai-me no orinpikku wa, Girisha **de** hirakaremashita.
The first Olympiad was held in Greece.

> ⌕ で (de) is also used when the place referred to is not a physical location (e.g., a conference room) so much as an occasion or situation (e.g., a conference).

i) 田村議員が、議会で質問した。
Tamura giin ga, gikai **de** shitsumon shita.
Assemblyperson Tamura asked a question in the Assembly/Parliament.

ii) 私は、あの会社の面接で、うまく答えられなかったので、入社できないかもしれない。
Watashi wa, ano kaisha no mensetsu **de**, umaku kotaerarenakatta no de, nyūsha dekinai ka mo shirenai.
At the employment interview for that company, I wasn't able to answer the questions very well, so I may not be accepted (may not be able to join the company).

2a. に (ni). Indicates where something is or exists, and is often combined with the verbs ある (aru; mostly in reference to inanimate objects) and いる (iru; mostly for animate objects). Compared with で (de; II-1), which also indicates the location of an action, に here indicates the location of an action that is relatively static rather than one that is dynamic. English equivalent: "in."

i) 私の両親の家は、東京にあります。
Watashi no ryōshin no ie wa, Tōkyō **ni** arimasu.
My parents' home is in Tokyo.

ii) ボールペンはその机の上にありますよ。
Bōrupen wa sono tsukue no ue **ni** arimasu yo.
The ball-point pen is right there on the desk.

iii) 戸田：部長は今どこにいますか？
川口：出張で、今日は九州にいるはずですよ。

Toda: Buchō wa ima doko **ni** imasu ka?
Kawaguchi: Shutchō de, kyō wa Kyūshū **ni** iru hazu desu yo.

Toda: Where is the department head right now?
Kawaguchi: On a business trip. Today he should be in Kyushu.

✐ When the subject is an event or happening (such as a parade), the location is most often indicated by で (de), not に (ni), even when the verb is いる (iru) or ある (aru).

i) 毎年、隅田川で花火大会があります。
Mainen (maitoshi), Sumida-gawa **de** hanabi-taikai ga arimasu.
Every year there is a fireworks display at the Sumida River.

ii) 今晩、銀座でパレードがあるそうです。
Konban, Ginza **de** parēdo ga aru sō desu.
This evening there is a parade in Ginza, they say.

2b. に (ni). Indicates a goal when used with verbs showing an inward movement. へ (e) can replace に (ni) in this usage, but に is more common. English equivalent: "in," "into."

i) あの大学にどうしても、入りたいんです。
Ano daigaku **ni** dōshite mo, hairitai n' desu.
No matter what, I want to get into that university.

ii) 夢の中に武君が出てきたんだって？
Yume no naka **ni** Takeshi-kun ga dete kita n' datte?
Is it true (as I heard) that Takeshi appeared in your dreams?

iii) 8階まで行くのに、エスカレーターよりエレベーターに乗ったほうが早いです。
Hachikai made iku no ni, esukarētā yori erebētā **ni** notta hō ga hayai desu.
To get to the eighth floor, it is faster to take the elevator than the escalator.

2c. に (ni). Indicates the location where an action takes place when combined with the following verbs: 座る (suwaru; to sit), 置く (oku; to put), 住む (sumu; to live, reside), 勤める (tsutomeru; to work), 積もる (tsumoru; to pile up). Compare this with で (de; II-1), which has the same function with most other verbs. English equivalent: "in," "on."

i) そのソファーに座って、お待ちください。
Sono sofā **ni** suwatte, omachi kudasai.
Please take a seat on that sofa and wait.

ii) すみませんが、鞄はそこにおいてください。
Sumimasen ga, kaban wa soko **ni** oite kudasai.
Excuse me, but could you put your bag/briefcase over there?

iii) 将来、田舎に住みたい。
Shōrai, inaka **ni** sumitai.
In the future I want to live out in the countryside.

iv) 滝川さんは、郵便局に勤めています。
Takigawa-san wa, yūbinkyoku **ni** tsutomete imasu.
Takigawa-san works in a post office.

v) ずいぶん屋根に雪が積もりましたね。
Zuibun yane **ni** yuki ga tsumorimashita ne.
The snow has really piled up on the roof, hasn't it.

3. の (no). In indicating a location, の is often combined with words such as 上 (ue; top), 下 (shita; bottom), 横 (yoko; beside), 中 (naka; inside), そば (soba; beside), and まえ (mae; front of) to give a more detailed description of the location.

i) あの山の上の展望台に行ってみよう。
Ano yama **no ue no** tenbōdai ni itte miyō.
Let's go up to the observation platform on that mountaintop.

ii) 学校の前の喫茶店で待っています。
Gakkō **no mae no** kissaten de matte imasu.
I'll be waiting at the coffee shop in front of the school.

iii) 駅の横の本屋で、この本を買いました。
Eki **no yoko no** hon'ya de, kono hon o kaimashita.
I bought this book at the bookstore beside the station.

4. へ／に (e/ni). Indicate the place toward which something is moving. へ and に are interchangeable when combined with such verbs as 行く (iku; to go), 来る (kuru; to come), 戻る (modoru; to come back), and 帰る (kaeru; to return). English equivalent: "in," "at."

i) 昼はあの店へ／に行って食事をしよう。
Hiru wa ano mise **e/ni** itte shokuji o shiyō.
For lunch, let's go and eat at that restaurant.

ii) 最近香港や韓国へ／に買い物に行く女性が多い。
Saikin Honkon ya Kankoku **e/ni** kaimono ni iku josei ga ōi.
Recently a lot of women go to Hong Kong and South Korea for shopping.

QUIZ II

QUIZ II-1

Choose the correct particle from among those appearing in parentheses. Answers are at the end of the quiz, along with English translations.

1. 知美：夏休みどうするの？
   頼子：できれば、スイス(へ｜で｜を｜が)行きたいと思ってる。
   Tomomi: Natsu-yasumi dō suru no?
   Yoriko: Dekireba, Suisu (e | de | o | ga) ikitai to omotte 'ru.

2. 正：これから何しようか？
   明代：お天気がいいから、公園(に｜へ｜で｜も)ボート(を｜が｜に｜へ)乗らない？
   Tadashi: Kore kara nani shiyō ka?
   Akiyo: Otenki ga ii kara, kōen (ni | e | de | mo) bōto (o | ga | ni | e) noranai?

3. 竹子：その新しいバッグ、どこ(に｜を｜へ｜で)買ったの？
   真澄：新宿(で｜に｜が｜の)ある新しい店よ。
   Takeko: Sono atarashii baggu, doko (ni | o | e | de) katta no?
   Masumi: Shinjuku (de | ni | ga | no) aru atarashii mise yo.

4. 竹村：明日の会議はどこ(も｜に｜へ｜で)やるの？
   青木：3階の会議室です。

Takemura: Ashita no kaigi wa doko (mo | ni | e | de) yaru no?
Aoki: Sangai no kaigishitsu desu.

5. 亜希子：ジョンって、どこ(に｜へ｜を｜で)生まれたのかしら。
   美保：知らなかったの？　日本生まれなのよ。
   Akiko: Jon tte, doko (ni | e | o | de) umareta no kashira.
   Miho: Shiranakatta no? Nihon-umare na no yo.

6. 太郎：どこ(へ｜を｜が｜の)行くの？
   元子：スーパー(で｜を｜に｜へ)買い物をしてこようと思うの。
   Tarō: Doko (e | o | ga | no) iku no?
   Motoko: Sūpā (de | o | ni | e) kaimono o shite koyō to omou no.

7. 毎年この大学(に｜へ｜が｜で)は、秋に学園祭がありますよ。
   Mainen (maitoshi) kono daigaku (ni | e | ga | de) wa, aki ni gakuensai ga arimasu yo.

8. 春子：富士山(で｜に｜の｜が)登ったことある？
   昭：ないんだよ。
   Haruko: Fuji-san (de | ni | no | ga) nobotta koto aru?
   Akira: Nai n' da yo.

9. 父：徹、どこ(が｜の｜へ｜に)いる？
   母：さっきまで、部屋(で｜に｜へ｜を)勉強していましたけど…
   Chichi: Tōru, doko (ga | no | e | ni) iru?
   Haha: Sakki made, heya (de | ni | e | o) benkyō shite imashita kedo ….

10. 武田さんは外国の銀行(を｜で｜へ｜に)勤めています。
    Takeda-san wa gaikoku no ginkō (o | de | e | ni) tsutomete imasu.

Answers and Translations for Quiz II-1

1 = へ (e). Tomomi: What're you doing during summer vacation? Yoriko: If I can, I'm thinking of going to Switzerland. / If possible, I'd really like to go to Switzerland.
2 = で (de), に (ni). Tadashi: What should we do now? Akiyo: The weather is good, so how about going for a boat ride in the park?
3 = で (de), に (ni). Takeko: Where'd you buy that new bag? Masumi: At a new store in Shinjuku.
4 = で (de). Takemura: Where're we going to have tomorrow's meeting? Aoki: In the conference room on the third floor.
5 = で (de). Akiko: Where was John born? Miho: You don't know? He was born in Japan.
6 = へ (e), で (de). Taro: Where're you going? Motoko: I think I'll go to the supermarket and do some shopping.
7 = で (de). Every year, in fall, a school festival is held at this university.
8 = に (ni). Haruko: Have you ever climbed Mt. Fuji? Akira: No, I haven't.
9 = に (ni), で (de). Father: Where's Toru? Mother: Well, he was studying in his room until a few minutes ago.
10 = に (ni). Takeda-san is working in a foreign bank.

III

Particles Showing Connections between Words

1. と (to)
2. も (mo)
3. も…も (mo … mo)
4. や (ya)
5. や…や…など (ya … ya … nado)
6. に (ni)
7. とか (to ka)
8. やら (yara)
9. て (-te)
10a-b. たり…たり (-tari … -tari)
11. ては (-te wa)

> ✐ Compare Group XI, which looks at some of these same particles from the perspective of presenting lists of similar items.

1. と (to). Indicates a connection between nouns that form a list of two or more items. The list is complete; that is, there are no other items that could be added to it (which contrasts to some of the other particles given in this section, which present partial lists that could be added to if the speaker chose to do so). に (ni; III-6) is similar to と in that it presents a complete list, but it has a more formal sound to it. English equivalent: "and."

i) 教室には、先生と生徒がいます。
Kyōshitsu ni wa sensei **to** seito ga imasu.
There are students and a teacher in the classroom.

ii) 大統領と副大統領がその会議に出席した。
Daitōryō **to** fuku-daitōryō ga sono kaigi ni shusseki shita.
The President and the Vice President attended that meeting.

2. も (mo). Indicates that the noun it follows is connected (or similar) in some way to something else already mentioned. The first item was not followed by も; the second item is. Compare this with も…も (mo … mo; III-3), where both of the items to be mentioned are given in the same sentence and each is followed by も. English equivalent: "also," "too."

i) 山田さんは、来月米国へ行きます。私も近いうちに行くつもりです。
Yamada-san wa raigetsu Beikoku e ikimasu. Watashi **mo** chikai uchi ni iku tsumori desu.
Yamada-san is going to the United States next month. I also plan to go before long.

ii) 弘子：明日のコンサート、香も来るの？
美保：香は来ないわ。

Hiroko: Ashita no konsāto, Kaori **mo** kuru no?
Miho: Kaori wa konai wa.

Hiroko: Is Kaori also coming to the concert tomorrow?
Miho: No, she won't be coming.

3. も…も (mo … mo). Like と (to; III-1), も…も indicates that a connection exists between nouns that form a complete list of two or more items, but unlike と, も…も places emphasis on each of the items. It is identical to も (mo; III-2) except that here both items are followed by も, whereas in III-2 only the second item is followed by も. English equivalent: "both."

i) 私はみかんもりんごも好きです。
Watashi wa mikan **mo** ringo **mo** suki desu.
I like both mikan oranges and apples.

ii) この手紙を松本さんにも、谷さんにも、送るつもりだ。
Kono tegami o Matsumoto-san ni **mo**, Tani-san ni **mo**, okuru tsumori da.

I intend to send this letter both to Matsumoto-san and to Tani-san.

4. や (ya). Indicates that a connection exists between two or more nouns that form a list of items. や is therefore similar to と (to) and も…も (mo ... mo), but it is different in that the list could be added to if the speaker wished to do so: that is, the list is only a partial list. English equivalent: " ... and ... and ... and such" or "things like ... and ...."

> i) 彼は昨晩、ビールや日本酒をかなり飲んだらしい。
> Kare wa sakuban, bīru **ya** nihonshu o kanari nonda rashii.
> Last night he apparently drank a lot of beer, sake, and other stuff.

> ii) 昨日買い物に行って、セーターや靴を買った。
> Kinō kaimono ni itte, sētā **ya** kutsu o katta.
> Yesterday I went shopping and bought a sweater, shoes, and some other things.

5. や…や…など (ya ... ya ... nado). Indicates connections between nouns forming a list that could be added to if the speaker chose to do so. It is identical to や (ya; III-4), except for the inclusion of など ("et cetera," "and so forth"), which emphasizes the fact that the list is partial. English equivalent: " ... and ... et cetera."

> i) 宴会の料理は、天ぷらや、すしや、さしみなどだった。
> Enkai no ryōri wa, tenpura **ya**, sushi **ya**, sashimi **nado** datta.
> The food at the party was tempura, sushi, sashimi, etc.

> ii) 昨夜のコンサートの曲目は、シューマンやショパンやシューベルトなどだった。
> Sakuya no konsāto no kyokumoku wa, Shūman **ya** Shopan **ya** Shūberuto **nado** datta.
> The music at the last night's concert included Schumann, Chopin, and Schubert.

6. に (ni). Like と (to; III-1), indicates a connection between two or more nouns to form a list that is complete in itself (unless, of course, the list ends with など [nado, "et cetera"; III-5], as in the second example below), but this particle differs from と in that it has a formal resonance. English equivalent: "and."

> i) 田中：この大学には、どんな有名な教授がいるんですか？
> 鈴木：そうですね、経済学部の藤原教授に、法学部の田原教授に、理学部の湯川教授でしょうか。

Tanaka: Kono daigaku ni wa, donna yūmei na kyōju ga iru n' desu ka?
Suzuki: Sō desu ne, keizaigakubu no Fujiwara kyōju **ni**, hōgakubu no Tahara kyōju **ni**, rigakubu no Yukawa kyōju deshō ka.

Tanaka: What famous professors are there at this university?
Suzuki: Well, I suppose that would be Professor Fujiwara of the economics faculty, Professor Tahara of the law faculty, and Professor Yukawa of the science faculty.

> ii) 客：今日はどんな料理がおすすめですか？
> ウエートレス：ますにヒラメなどの魚料理はいかがですか？

Kyaku: Kyō wa donna ryōri ga osusume desu ka?
Uētoresu: Masu **ni** hirame nado no sakana ryōri wa ikaga desu ka?

Customer: What do you recommend today?
Waitress: How about fish, such as trout and flatfish?

7. とか (to ka). Indicates a connection between nouns, adjectives, and verbs to form a partial list of examples that could be added to if the speaker wished to do so. In that way, it is similar to や (ya; III-4), but it is different in that it is more casual and in that や only connects nouns. とか is also similar to だの (dano; XI-3) in casually connecting nouns, adjectives, and verbs in a partial list; however, with だの the items given in the list often have a negative impact. とか is often followed by the verb する at the end of the clause or sentence, which is also the case with たり…たり (-tari … -tari; III-10). English equivalent: "and ... and ... and so on."

i) 休みの日には、家で本を読む**とか**、テレビを観る**とか**しています。
Yasumi no hi ni wa, ie de hon o yomu **to ka**, terebi o miru **to ka** shite imasu.
I spend my holidays at home reading books, watching TV, and stuff.

ii) 孝：学生時代にどんな本を読みましたか？
光子：そうですね。夏目漱石**とか**、芥川龍之介**とか**はよく読みましたね。

Takashi: Gakusei jidai ni donna hon o yomimashita ka?
Mitsuko: Sō desu ne. Natsume Sōseki **to ka**, Akutagawa Ryūnosuke **to ka** wa yoku yomimashita ne.

Takashi: What kind of books did you read when you were a student?
Mitsuko: Let me see. I read a lot of Soseki Natsume and Ryunosuke Akutagawa and so on.

8. やら (yara). Connects nouns, adjectives, and verbs in a partial list. It is similar to とか (to ka; III-7) in this respect but different in that the items it lists indicate a somewhat confused or disorganized state of affairs. English equivalent: "... and ... and who knows what."

i) 由香：京都旅行どうだった？
珠美：面白かったわよ。でもお寺**やら**、神社**やら**、たくさん観て疲れたわ。

Yuka: Kyōto-ryokō dō datta?
Tamami: Omoshirokatta wa yo. Demo otera **yara**, jinja **yara**, takusan mite tsukareta wa.

Yuka: How was the trip to Kyoto?
Tamami: It was interesting. But I saw so many temples, shrines, and stuff that I got tired.

ii) 健二：昨日飲んだ？
義彦：ウィスキー**やら**、焼酎**やら**、ビール**やら**飲んで、今日はひどい二日酔いだよ。

Kenji: Kinō nonda?
Yoshihiko: Uisukī **yara**, shōchū **yara**, bīru **yara** nonde, kyō wa hidoi futsuka-yoi da yo.

Kenji: Did you drink yesterday?
Yoshihiko: What with drinking whiskey, *shochu*, beer, and who knows what, I've got a terrible hangover today.

9. て (-te form). Connects two or more verbs or adjectives that are similar in grammatical function and that present a complete list of two or more items that cannot be added to. This contrasts with the particles III-7–10, which play a role in presenting partial lists. The て form can also indicate a reason or cause (see VI-1). English equivalent: "and."

i) 空が青く**て**、太陽が輝いている。
Sora ga aoku**te**, taiyō ga kagayaite iru.
The sky is blue and the sun is shining.

ii) 明日はデパートで買い物をし**て**映画をみようと思っています。
Ashita wa depāto de kaimono o shi**te** eiga o miyō to omotte imasu.
Tomorrow I'm thinking of shopping at a department store and going to see a movie.

10a. たり…たり (-tari ... -tari). Indicates that two or more verbs or adjectives have the same grammatical function and are connected by the たり form to constitute one set. In this way, it is similar to the て (-te) form discussed in III-9 in connecting verbs or adjectives, but it is different in that this form hints that there are other verbs or adjectives which could be added to the list if one wished to. たり…たり is often followed by the verb する (suru), and in this respect is similar to とか (to ka; III-7). The たり form is made by adding り to the plain past form of a verb or adjective. English equivalent: "and ... etc."

i) 日曜日は、ゴルフをし**たり**、テニスをし**たり**して過ごします。
Nichiyōbi wa, gorufu o shi**tari**, tenisu o shi**tari** shite sugoshimasu.
I spend Sundays playing golf, tennis, and doing other stuff.

ii) 旅行中は、美術館に行っ**たり**、お土産を買っ**たり**しました。
Ryokō-chū wa, bijutsukan ni it**tari**, omiyage o kat**tari** shimashita.
On the trip I did things like go to museums and buy presents to take back home.

10b. たり…たり (-tari ... -tari). Indicates that two verbs or adjectives are connected to show a repetition of opposite actions or effects. This is similar to ては (-te wa; III-11) in connecting verbs, but in たり…たり the verbs are not as tightly bound in terms of time or cause and effect.

i) 今週は寒かっ**たり**、暑かっ**たり**します。
Konshū wa samukat**tari**, atsukat**tari** shimasu.
This week, it's been hot and cold, hot and cold.

ii) そんなに窓を開け**たり**閉め**たり**しないでくれる？
Sonna ni mado o ake**tari** shime**tari** shinai de kureru?
Could you stop opening and closing the window like that?

11. ては (-te wa). Connects two verbs whose actions are repeated and follow closely on one another. This closeness differentiates ては from たり…たり (-tari … -tari; III-10b), which can also show repeated actions. ては is also often followed by the verb する (suru). English equivalent: "and."

i) 最近仕事が忙しくて、休日は疲れて、食べ**ては**寝、食べ**ては**寝、するだけです。
Saikin shigoto ga isogashikute, kyūjitsu wa tsukarete, tabe**te wa** ne, tabe**te wa** ne, suru dake desu.
These days I am so busy, and I am tired on the holidays, so I just eat and sleep, eat and sleep.

ii) 赤ちゃんは、ミルクを飲ん**では**寝、寝**ては**飲んで、だんだん大きくなっていくんですね。
Akachan wa, miruku o non**de wa** ne, ne**te wa** nonde, dandan ōkiku natte iku n' desu ne.
The baby drinks its milk and goes to sleep, goes to sleep and drinks its milk, and little by little grows bigger.

QUIZ III

QUIZ III–1

Choose the correct particle from among those appearing below the sample sentences. Answers are to be found at the end of the quiz, along with English translations.

1. スーパーでりんご(　　)みかんを買った。
   Sūpā de ringo (　　) mikan o katta.

   1. を (o)　2. たり (-tari … -tari)　3. と (to)　4. も (mo)

2. 昨日友達の家で、食べ(　　)飲んだりした。
   Kinō tomodachi no ie de, tabe (　　) nondari shita.

   1. と (to)　2. ても (-te mo)　3. たり (-tari)　4. やら (yara)

3. 山に登った時は、疲れ(　　)空腹(　　)で、死にそうだった。
   Yama ni nobotta toki wa, tsukare (　　) kūfuku (　　) de, shinisō datta.

   1. に (ni)　2. も (mo)　3. やら (yara)　4. たり (-tari)

4. フランスでは、美術館や城(　　)を見た。
   Furansu de wa, bijutsukan ya shiro (　　) o mita.

   1. など (nado)　2. や (ya)　3. も (mo)　4. て (-te)

5. この道路は、大きい車が行ったり来（　　）している。
   Kono dōro wa, ōkī kuruma ga ittari ki (　　) shite iru.

   1. ては (-te wa)　2. て (-te)　3. たり (-tari)　4. やら (yara)

6. 私の大学には、アメリカ（　　）、フランスや、中国などからの外国人学生もいます。
   Watashi no daigaku ni wa, Amerika (　　), Furansu ya, Chūgoku nado kara no gaikokujin-gakusei mo imasu.

   1. も (mo)　2. やら (yara)　3. と (to)　4. や (ya)

7. あの人は、食べ（　　）飲み、飲んでは食べ、しています。
   Ano hito wa, tabe (　　) nomi, nonde wa tabe, shite imasu.

   1. たり (-tari)　2. ては (-te wa)　3. て (-te)　4. と (to)

8. 朝食は、サラダにトースト（　　）コーヒーでした。
   Chōshoku wa, sarada ni tōsuto (　　) kōhī deshita.

   1. やら (yara)　2. と (to)　3. も (mo)　4. に (ni)

9. この論文は難しいので、少し読んでは考え、考え（　　）読むようにしています。
   Kono ronbun wa muzukashii no de, sukoshi yonde wa kangae, kangae (　　) yomu yō ni shite imasu.

   1. たり (-tari)　2. ては (-te wa)　3. て (-te)　4. も (mo)

10. すし（　　）日本酒、それが一番いい組み合わせですね。
    Sushi (　　) Nihonshu, sore ga ichiban ii kumiawase desu ne.

    1. に (ni)　2. も (mo)　3. と (to)　4. や (ya)

Answers and Translations for Quiz III-1

1 = 3. At the supermarket I bought apples and mikan oranges.
2 = 3. Yesterday I ate, drank, and whatnot at a friend's home.
3 = 3, 3. When we climbed the mountain, I was tired, hungry, and stuff, and just about to die.
4 = 1. In France, I saw museums, castles, and so on.
5 = 3. There are large vehicles going up and down this street.
6 = 4. At my university, there are exchange students from America, France, China, and other countries.
7 = 2. That person just eats and drinks, drinks and eats.
8 = 4. Breakfast was salad, toast, and coffee.
9 = 2. This report is hard, so I read a bit and think about it, and after thinking about it, read some more.
10 = 1. Sushi and Japanese sake, that's the best combo there is.

QUIZ III-2

Choose the correct particle from among those appearing in parentheses. Answers are to be found at the end of the quiz, along with English translations.

1. 母：果物のジャムを2種類作るんだけど、いちご（と｜や）りんごでいいかしら？
   娘：いいわね。
   Haha: Kudamono no jamu o ni-shurui tsukuru n' da kedo, ichigo (to | ya) ringo de ii kashira?
   Musume: Ii wa ne.

2. 知子：明日渋谷へ買い物に行く予定なの。光代（や｜も）行かない？
   光代：行く、行く。
   Tomoko: Ashita Shibuya e kaimono ni iku yotei na no. Mitsuyo (ya | mo) ikanai?
   Mitsuyo: Iku, iku.

3. 昨日本屋へ行って、経済の本（も｜や）、経営の本や、政治の本（など｜も）を買った。
   Kinō hon'ya e itte, keizai no hon (mo | ya), keiei no hon ya, seiji no hon (nado | ya) o katta.

4. 日曜日は買い物をし（やら｜たり）、展覧会を観たりして過ごした。
   Nichiyōbi wa kaimono o shi (yara | -tari), tenrankai o mitari shite sugoshita.

5. 赤ちゃんは、目を覚まし（ては｜たり）ミルクを飲み、ミルクを飲んでは眠っている。
   Akachan wa, me o samashi (-te wa | -tari) miruku o nomi, miruku o nonde wa nemutte iru.

6. 旅行に行く人は、竹内さんに、大石さん（と｜に）、川村さんです。
   Ryokō ni iku hito wa, Takeuchi-san ni, Ōishi-san (to | ni), Kawamura-san desu.

7. 秋子：去年のヨーロッパ旅行、どんな国に行ったの？
   香：フランス（や｜とか）、スイス（とか｜も）、イタリアとか、スペインとか…
   Akiko: Kyonen no Yōroppa-ryokō, donna kuni ni itta no?
   Kaori: Furansu (ya | to ka), Suisu (to ka | mo), Itaria to ka, Supein to ka …

8. 係長：A案（と｜が）B案がありますが、安田さんはどちらが面白いと思いますか？
   安田：難しいですね。A案（と｜も）、B案（も｜やら）それぞれ面白いので…
   Kakarichō: A-an (to | ga) B-an ga arimasu ga, Yasuda-san wa dochira ga omoshiroi to omoimasu ka?
   Yasuda: Muzukashii desu ne. A-an (to | mo), B-an (mo | yara) sorezore omoshiroi no de …

9. 春になると、この辺は梅(と ｜ や)、桃や、桜(とか ｜ など)、ピンクの花がきれいに咲きます。
   Haru ni naru to, kono hen wa ume (to | ya), momo ya, sakura (to ka | nado), pinku no hana ga kirei ni sakimasu.

10. 北海道には、鮭(やら ｜ と)、じゃがいもやら、とうもろこし(も ｜ など)、おいしい食べ物がたくさんある。
    Hokkaidō ni wa, sake (yara | to), jagaimo yara, tōmorokoshi (mo | nado), oishii tabemono ga takusan aru.

Answers and Translations for Quiz III-2

1 = と (to). Mother: I'm going to make two kinds of fruit jam. Does strawberry and apple sound okay? Daughter: Sounds good to me.

2 = も (mo). Tomoko: Tomorrow I plan to go to Shibuya to shop. Do you want to go too? Mitsuyo: Sure I do.

3 = や (ya), など (nado). I went to a bookstore yesterday and bought a book on economics, a book on management, a book on politics, and some others.

4 = たり (-tari). I spent Sunday doing some shopping, going to an exhibition, and other things.

5 = ては (-te wa). The baby wakes up to drink its milk, and when it's had its milk, goes back to sleep.

6 = に (ni). The people going on the trip are Takeuchi-san, Ōishi-san, and Kawamura-san.

7 = とか (to ka), とか (to ka). Akiko: On your trip to Europe last year, what countries did you go to? Kaori: France, Switzerland, Italy, Spain, and some others.

8 = と (to), も (mo), も (mo). Section Chief: We have two plans, Yasuda-san, A and B. Which do you think is more interesting? Yasuda: That's a hard one. Both plan A and plan B are interesting in their own way.

9 = や (ya), など (nado). When spring comes round, all kinds of pretty pink flowers bloom around here, like plums, peaches, cherries.

10 = やら (yara), など (nado). There are a lot of good things to eat in Hokkaido, like salmon, potatoes, and corn.

IV

Particles that Indicate Direction

1. に／へ (ni/e)
2. から (kara)
3. から…まで (kara … made)
4. より (yori)

1. に／へ (ni/e). Indicates the direction toward which something is moving. In this sense に and へ are interchangeable. English equivalent: "to."

i) 歩いて駅に／へ行きます。
Aruite eki **ni/e** ikimasu.
I will walk to the station.

ii) 銀座に／へ行くには、地下鉄が便利でしょう。
Ginza **ni/e** iku ni wa, chikatetsu ga benri deshō.
The subway is probably most convenient to go to Ginza.

iii) 柳田さんに／へメールを送った。
Yanagida-san **ni/e** mēru o okutta.
I sent an email to Yanagida-san.

iv) 明日は何時に空港に／へ行けばいいんですか？
Ashita wa nanji ni kūkō **ni/e** ikeba ii n' desu ka?
What time should I be at (go to) the airport tomorrow?

2. から (kara). Indicates the point from which an action starts. より (yori; IV-4) has the same function but is used in more formal or official situations. English equivalent: "from."

   i) 今、会社**から**帰ったところです。
      Ima, kaisha **kara** kaetta tokoro desu.
      I just now returned from the office.

   ii) 昨晩、何時ごろ友達**から**電話がありましたか？
      Sakuban, nanji goro tomodachi **kara** denwa ga arimashita ka?
      About what time was it last night that there was a call from my friend?

3. から…まで (kara … made). Indicates the starting place and ending place of an action. English equivalent: "from … to."

   i) 松本：駅**から**ホテル**まで**は、何分ぐらいかかりますか？
     駅員：5分ぐらいですよ。

     Matsumoto: Eki **kara** hoteru **made** wa, nanpun gurai kakarimasu ka?
     Eki-in: Gofun gurai desu yo.

     Matsumoto: About how long (how many minutes) does it take from the station to the hotel?
     Station attendant: About five minutes.

   ii) ホノルル**から**横浜**まで**、船で帰りました。
      Honoruru **kara** Yokohama **made**, fune de kaerimashita.
      I came back from Honolulu to Yokohama by boat.

4. より (yori). Indicates the starting point of an action; more formal or official-sounding than から (kara; IV-2). English equivalent: "from."

   i) さくらホテルは、駅の東口**より**歩いて5分。

Sakura hoteru wa, eki no higashi-guchi **yori** aruite gofun.
On foot, the Sakura Hotel is five minutes from the east exit of the station.

ii) 来週は、関西**より**九州に移動の予定です。
Raishū wa, Kansai **yori** Kyūshū ni idō no yotei desu.
Next week, the schedule calls for me/us to move (travel) from Kansai to Kyushu.

QUIZ IV

QUIZ IV-1

Choose the correct particle from among those appearing below the sample sentences. Answers are to be found at the end of the quiz, along with English translations.

1. 昨日は米国に帰国する友人を、ホテルから空港(　　)車で送った。
   Kinō wa Beikoku ni kikoku suru yūjin o, hoteru kara kūkō (　　) kuruma de okutta.

   1. より (yori)　2. から (kara)　3. まで (made)　4. までに (made ni)

2. 夏休みには、ハワイかグアム(　　)行こうと思っている。
   Natsu-yasumi ni wa, Hawai ka Guamu (　　) ikō to omotte iru.

   1. へ (e)　2. まで (made)　3. より (yori)　4. から (kara)

3. これが今朝、法律事務所(　　)届いた書類だ。
   Kore ga kesa, hōritsu-jimusho (　　) todoita shorui da.

   1. まで (made)　2. より (yori)　3. とか (to ka)　4. で (de)

4. あのデパート(　　)行くのに、バスと電車とどちらが便利でしょうか？
   Ano depāto (　　) iku no ni, basu to densha to dochira ga benri deshō ka?

1. より (yori)   2. まで (made)   3. にも (ni mo)   4. から (kara)

5. 来週は松山から、熊本（　　）行かなければならない。
   Raishū wa Matsuyama kara, Kumamoto (　　) ikanakereba naranai.

   1. まで (made)   2. より (yori)   3. とか (to ka)   4. から (kara)

6. 真智子：そんなに急いで、どこ（　　）行くのよ？
   時子：駅。5時の電車に乗りたいの。
   Machiko: Sonna ni isoide, doko (　　) iku no yo?
   Tokiko: Eki. Goji no densha ni noritai no.

   1. より (yori)   2. から (kara)   3. へ (e)   4. も (mo)

7. 明日は、父が海外出張（　　）帰ってくる予定です。
   Ashita wa, chichi ga kaigai-shutchō (　　) kaette kuru yotei desu.

   1. へ (e)   2. も (mo)   3. に (ni)   4. から (kara)

8. さっきから、家の前をパトカーや消防車が、駅の方（　　）走っていきますが、何かあったのでしょうか？
   Sakki kara, ie no mae o patokā ya shōbōsha ga, eki no hō (　　) hashitte ikimasu ga, nani ka atta no deshō ka?

   1. より (yori)   2. へ (e)   3. から (kara)   4. までに (made ni)

9. 昨日山本さん（　　）メールを送ったが、まだ返事が来ない。
   Kinō Yamamoto-san (　　) mēru o okutta ga, mada henji ga konai.

   1. に (ni)   2. から (kara)   3. より (yori)   4. まで (made)

10. あの新しいビルの屋上（　　）、富士山がきれいに見えます。
    Ano atarashii biru no okujō (　　), Fuji-san ga kirei ni miemasu.

    1. へ (e)   2. まで (made)   3. までに (made ni)   4. から (kara)

QUIZ IV

Answers and Translations for Quiz IV-1

1 = 3. Yesterday I sent off a friend returning to the United States, taking her from the hotel to the airport by car.
2 = 1. This summer vacation I am thinking of going to either Hawaii or Guam.
3 = 2. These are the papers that arrived from the law office this morning.
4 = 2. Bus or train, which is more convenient to get to that department store?
5 = 1. Next week I have to go from Matsuyama to Kumamoto.
6 = 3. Machiko: Where do you think you're going in such a hurry? Tokiko: The station. I want to catch the five o'clock train.
7 = 4. Tomorrow my father is scheduled to return from an overseas business trip.
8 = 2. For a while now police cars and fire engines have been going past the house toward the station. I wonder if something has happened.
9 = 1. Yesterday I sent an email to Yamamoto-san, but haven't gotten an answer yet.
10 = 4. You can get a beautiful view of Mt. Fuji from the roof of that new building.

QUIZ IV-2

Choose the correct particle from among those appearing in parentheses. Answers are at the end of the quiz, along with English translations.

1. 林：ご相談したいことがあるので、明日、会社 (に ｜ も) 伺ってもいいでしょうか？
   横田：ええ、どうぞ。
   Hayashi: Gosōdan shitai koto ga aru no de, ashita, kaisha (ni | mo) ukagatte mo ii deshō ka?
   Yokota: Ee, dōzo.

2. 毎日運動のために、家 (へ ｜ から) 会社まで歩いています。
   Mainichi undō no tame ni, ie (e | kara) kaisha made aruite imasu.

3. 結果がわかったら、すぐ私 (より ｜ に) 電話をくれませんか？
   Kekka ga wakattara, sugu watashi (yori | ni) denwa o kuremasen ka?

4. 社長は、午後、九州（から｜まで）東京に戻られる予定。
   Shachō wa, gogo, Kyūshū (kara | made) Tōkyō ni modorareru yotei.

5. 尚子：札幌雪祭りに行ったんだって？
   由美：きれいだったわ。雪祭りを見て、札幌（に｜から）バスで小樽まで行ったのよ。
   Naoko: Sapporo-yukimatsuri ni itta n' datte?
   Yumi: Kirei datta wa. Yukimatsuri o mite, Sapporo (ni | kara) basu de Otaru made itta no yo.

6. 武田：今日の飛行機で大阪へ行くんだろう？
   広崎：その予定なんだ。ここ（へ｜から）羽田まで、何分くらいかかるだろうね。
   Takeda: Kyō no hikōki de Ōsaka e iku n' darō?
   Hirosaki: Sono yotei nan da. Koko (e | kara) Haneda made, nan-pun kurai kakaru darō ne.

7. 明日の国際会議には、世界中（より｜へ）代表が集まるそうです。
   Ashita no kokusai-kaigi ni wa, sekai-jū (yori | e) daihyō ga atsumaru sō desu.

8. 亜紀：お母さん、どこ（へ｜から）行ったの？
   俊彦：スーパー（に｜から）買い物に行った。
   Aki: Okāsan, doko (e | kara) itta no?
   Toshihiko: Sūpā (ni | kara) kaimono ni itta.

9. 今朝、大学（から｜まで）合格の通知を受け取った。
   Kesa, daigaku (kara | made) gōkaku no tsūchi o uketotta.

10. 来週の土曜日の晩、コンサート（に｜より）行くつもりです。
    Raishū no doyōbi no ban, konsāto (ni | yori) iku tsumori desu.

Answers and Translations for Quiz IV-2

1 = に (ni). Hayashi: I have something that I would like to discuss. Is it all right if I call at your office tomorrow? Yokota: Yes, please do.
2 = から (kara). To get some exercise, I walk every day from my home to the office.
3 = に (ni). Could you give me a call as soon as you know the results?
4 = から (kara). The President is scheduled to return to Tokyo from Kyushu in the afternoon.
5 = から (kara). Naoko: I hear you went to the Sapporo Snow Festival. Yumi: It was really lovely. After seeing the Snow Festival, I went from Sapporo to Otaru by bus.
6 = から (kara). Takeda: You're taking today's plane to Osaka, right? Hirosaki: That's the plan. How long (about how many minutes) does it take from here to Haneda (airport)?
7 = より (yori). At tomorrow's international conference, delegates are said to be assembling from around the world.
8 = へ (e), に (ni). Aki: Where has mother gone? Toshihiko: To the supermarket for some shopping.
9 = から (kara). I got an acceptance notification from the university this morning.
10 = に (ni). Next Saturday night, I plan to go to a concert.

V

Particles that Indicate a Question or Uncertainty

1a-b. か (ka)
2. かな (ka na)
3. かしら (kashira)
4. の (no)
5. って (tte)

1a. か (ka). Indicates a question at the end of a sentence. Its tone has the politeness expected in everyday conversation with strangers or social superiors, in contrast to the casualness indicated by particles V-2–5.

i) 山本：最近お仕事はいかがです**か**？
   竹下：以前ほど順調ではないですね。

   Yamamoto: Saikin oshigoto wa ikaga desu **ka**?
   Takeshita: Izen hodo junchō de wa nai desu ne.

   Yamamoto: How is work going these days?
   Takeshita: Not as smoothly as before.

ii) 京子：昨日の試合、どっちが勝ったんです**か**？
    直美：もちろんAチームですよ。

    Kyōko: Kinō no shiai, dotchi ga katta n' desu **ka**?
    Naomi: Mochiron A-chīmu desu yo.

    Kyoko: Who won yesterday's game?
    Naomi: The A team, of course.

1b. か (ka). Indicating a question, doubt, or uncertainty in mid-sentence.

i) 今日は風邪を引いたの**か**、朝からのどが痛い。
Kyō wa kaze o hiita no **ka**, asa kara nodo ga itai.
Maybe I've caught a cold—I've had a sore throat today since morning.

ii) 明日の会合に何人来るの**か**、わからない。
Ashita no kaigō ni nannin kuru no **ka**, wakaranai.
I don't know how many people are coming to tomorrow's gathering.

2. かな (ka na). Typically used by men, indicates a tentative question or uncertainty at the end of a sentence. The feminine equivalent is かしら (kashira; V-3), both in function and in casualness of tone. English equivalent: "I wonder."

i) 課長：午後からの緊急会議のこと、みんな知ってる**かな**？
係長：大丈夫ですよ、メールしてありますから…

Kachō: Gogo kara no kinkyū-kaigi no koto, minna shitte 'ru **ka na**?
Kakarichō: Daijōbu desu yo, mēru shite arimasu kara …

Section chief: I wonder if everyone knows about the emergency meeting starting this afternoon.
Subsection chief: Don't worry about it. An email has been sent out.

ii) 夫：明日ゴルフに行くんだけど、高田君も行かない**かな**？
妻：お電話してみたら？

Otto: Ashita gorufu ni iku n' da kedo, Takada-kun mo ikanai **ka na**?
Tsuma: Odenwa shite mitara?

Husband: I'm going golfing tomorrow. I wonder if Takada won't go too.
Wife: Why not call and find out?

3. かしら (kashira). Typically used by women, indicating a tentative question or uncertainty at the end of a sentence. The masculine equivalent is かな (ka na; V-2), both in function and in casualness of tone.

i) 妻：どうしたの**かしら**？　お財布に入れておいたのに、鍵がないの。
　　夫：大丈夫、テーブルの上にあるよ。

　Tsuma: Dō shita no **kashira**? Osaifu ni irete oita no ni, kagi ga nai no.
　Otto: Daijōbu, tēburu no ue ni aru yo.

　Wife: I wonder what happened? I put it in my purse, but the key is gone.
　Husband: Don't worry. It's there on the table.

ii) 智美：あの新しいレストラン、おいしい**かしら**？
　　美江：おいしいわよ。昨日百合と行ってみたの。

　Satomi: Ano atarashii resutoran, oishii **kashira**?
　Mie: Oishii wa yo. Kinō Yuri to itte mita no.

　Satomi: I wonder how good that new restaurant is?
　Mie: It's pretty good. Yesterday I went with Yuri to try it out.

4. の (no). Spoken with rising intonation, indicates a question at the end of the sentence. Equivalent in function to か (ka; V-1a) but provides a softer, more casual tone.

i) 母：もうご飯食べた**の**？
　　息子：まだ食べ終わってないよ。

　Haha: Mō gohan tabeta **no**?
　Musuko: Mada tabeowatte 'nai yo.

　Mother: Have you already eaten?
　Son: I haven't finished yet. / I'm still eating.

ii) 春美：どこへ行く**の**？
久美子：お茶飲みに行くんだけど、春美も行かない？

Harumi: Doko e iku **no**?
Kumiko: Ocha nomi ni iku n' da kedo, Harumi mo ikanai?

Harumi: Where are you going?
Kumiko: I'm going out for a cup of tea. Why don't you come along?

5. って (tte). With a rising intonation, indicates a question at the end of a sentence, asking if what one has heard is true. Typical of the spoken language and most often heard between friends or family. Often found in the form of だって (datte), but can also follow a verb (食べるって taberu tte). Without the rising intonation, the question becomes a statement (as in Tomiko's response in the second sentence below), meaning "I hear that...." English equivalent: "Is it true (as I have heard) that...?"

i) 由香：フランス語、明日試験だ**って**？
登美子：そうだって、いやねえ...

Yuka: Furansu-go, ashita shiken da**tte**?
Tomiko: Sō datte, iya nee...

Yuka: Is it true there's a French test tomorrow?
Tomiko: That's what I hear. Ugh!

ii) 高山：部長、もう帰っちゃったんだ**って**？
近藤：そうなんですよ。

Takayama: Buchō, mō kaetchatta n' da**tte**?
Kondō: Sō nan desu yo.

Takayama: The department head's already gone?
Kondo: That's correct.

QUIZ V

QUIZ V–1

Choose the correct particle from among those appearing below the sample sentences. Answers are at the end of the quiz, along with English translations.

1. 山田：この建物は、何年前に建てられたんです（　　）？
   高森：よくわかりませんが、100年ぐらい前だそうですよ。
   Yamada: Kono tatemono wa, nannen mae ni taterareta n' desu (　　)?
   Takamori: Yoku wakarimasen ga, hyakunen gurai mae da sō desu yo.

   1. って (tte)　2. か (ka)　3. ね (ne)

2. 由香：今日、洋も来る（　　）？
   俊子：来るって言ってたけど。
   Yuka: Kyō, Hiroshi mo kuru (　　)?
   Toshiko: Kuru tte itte 'ta kedo.

   1. よ (yo)　2. かしら (kashira)　3. か (ka)

3. 兄：そろそろバスが来る頃（　　）？
   弟：あと5分で来るよ。
   Ani: Sorosoro basu ga kuru koro (　　)?
   Otōto: Ato gofun de kuru yo.

   1. かな (ka na)　2. かしら (kashira)　3. も (mo)

4. 客：これはいくらです（　）？
   店員：それは2500円でございます。
   Kyaku: Kore wa ikura desu (　)?
   Ten'in: Sore wa nisengohyaku-en de gozaimasu.

   1. かな (ka na)　2. よ (yo)　3. か (ka)

5. 春美：あゆみ、怒ってる（　）？
   洋子：怒ってなんかいないと思うけど。
   Harumi: Ayumi, okotte 'ru (　)?
   Yōko: Okotte nanka inai to omou kedo.

   1. か (ka)　2. よ (yo)　3. かしら (kashira)

Answers and Translations for Quiz V-1

1 = 2. Yamada: How many years ago was this building constructed? Takamori: I'm not sure, but they say about 100 years ago.
2 = 2. Yuka: I wonder if Hiroshi's coming today? Toshiko: He said he would.
3 = 1. Older brother: The bus should be coming pretty soon, I guess. Younger brother: It'll be here in another five minutes.
4 = 3. Customer: How much is this? Clerk: That's ¥2,500.
5 = 3. Harumi: I wonder if Ayumi is mad? Yoko: I don't think she's mad or anything.

QUIZ V-1

Choose the correct particle from among those appearing in parentheses. Answers are at the end of the quiz, along with English translations.

1. 松尾：明日、何時に家を出たらいいでしょう（か｜の）？
   広谷：できれば6時に出てください。
   Matsuo: Ashita, nanji ni ie o detara ii deshō (ka | no)?
   Hirotani: Dekireba rokuji ni dete kudasai.

2. 雪子：元子さん、どこか具合が悪いんじゃない（って｜の）？
   元子：そうなのよ、頭が痛くて…
   Yukiko: Motoko-san, doko ka guai ga warui n' ja nai (tte | no)?
   Motoko: Sō na no yo, atama ga itakute …

3. 清美：今日は富士山が見える（かしら｜と）？
   良江：見えるといいわね、せっかく箱根に来たんだから。
   Kiyomi: Kyō wa Fuji-san ga mieru (kashira | to)?
   Yoshie: Mieru to ii wa ne, sekkaku Hakone ni kita n' da kara.

4. 課長：山本君、遅いね、どうしたの（かな｜か）？
   係長：本当にどうしたんでしょうね、連絡もないんですよ。
   Kachō: Yamamoto-kun, osoi ne, dō shita no (ka na | ka)?
   Kakarichō: Hontō ni dō shita n' deshō ne, renraku mo nai n' desu yo.

5. 司会者：今日の会議はこれで終わりたいと思いますが、何か質問はありません（の｜か）？
   Shikaisha: Kyō no kaigi wa kore de owaritai to omoimasu ga, nani ka shitsumon wa arimasen (no | ka)?

Answers and Translations for Quiz V-2

1 = か (ka). Matsuo: What time should I leave the house tomorrow? Hirotani: If possible, please leave at 6:00.
2 = の (no). Yukiko: Motoko, aren't you feeling well? Motoko: Not really. I've got this headache.
3 = かしら (kashira). Kiyomi: I wonder if we'll be able to see Mt. Fuji today. Yoshie: I hope so, after coming all the way to Hakone.
4 = かな (ka na). Section chief: Yamamoto's late. I wonder what's happened to him. Subsection chief: Really, what could have happened to him? And he hasn't called in either.
5 = か (ka). Chairperson: I would now like to bring today's meeting to an end. Are there any questions?

VI

Particles that Indicate a Reason or Cause

1. て (-te)
2. で (de)
3. から (kara)
4. ので (no de)
5. もので (mono de)

1. て (-te form). As the connection between two clauses, the て form of adjectives and verbs can indicate a reason at the end of the first clause in a sentence. Note that the て form can also mean "and" (see III-9). Telling the difference depends on reading the context correctly. English equivalents: "because," "since," "so."

i) 道が込んで**いて**、6時までに空港に行くのは無理だ。
   Michi ga konde i**te**, rokuji made ni kūkō ni iku no wa muri da.
   The roads are crowded, so it's impossible to get to the airport by 6:00.

ii) あそこは今雪が多く**て**、歩いていけませんよ。
   Asoko wa ima yuki ga ōku**te**, aruite ikemasen yo.
   Right now the snow is heavy there, so you can't go (get there) on foot.

2. で (de). Following nouns, indicates that the noun is the reason for the situation given in the following verb. で can sometimes be made softer in tone by converting it into ので (no de; VI-4) or more direct by replacing it with から (kara; VI-3). English equivalent: "due to," "owing to," "because of."

> i) 林さんは、病気で先週から会社を休んでいます。
> Hayashi-san wa, byōki **de** senshū kara kaisha o yasunde imasu.
> Because Hayashi-san has been ill, he has been away from the office since last week.

> ii) 今朝は、事故で電車が1時間も止まった。
> Kesa wa, jiko **de** densha ga ichiji-kan mo tomatta.
> This morning, due to an accident, the train stopped running for a whole hour.

3. から (kara). Indicates a reason and can follow a verb, adjective, na-adjective, or noun; nouns and na-adjective must be accompanied by だ (da) when they are used with から. Compared with ので (no de; VI-4) and もので (mono de; VI-5), から is much more direct in giving a cause or reason and is therefore often avoided in polite conversation when the "reason" may somehow offend the other party. English equivalent: "because."

> i) 久子：今悪い風邪がはやっているけど、お宅のお子さん大丈夫？
> 知美：ありがとう。うちの子、いつも元気だ**から**大丈夫よ。
>
> Hisako: Ima warui kaze ga hayatte iru kedo, otaku no okosan daijōbu?
> Tomomi: Arigatō. Uchi no ko, itsumo genki da **kara** daijōbu yo.
>
> Hisako: There is a bad cold going around now. Is your boy/girl OK?
> Tomomi: Thanks for asking. Our little boy/girl is always full of energy, so he/she should be OK.

> ii) 富山：午後, ゴルフに行かない？
> 稲葉：今日は雨だ**から**、明日にしようよ。

Toyama: Gogo, gorufu ni ikanai?
Inaba: Kyō wa ame da **kara**, ashita ni shiyō yo.

Toyama: Want to go golfing this afternoon?
Inaba: Since it's supposed to rain today, let's make it tomorrow.

4. ので (no de). Indicates a reason or cause at the end of a clause, the result of which is given in the following clause. Nouns and na-adjectives take な (na) before ので. ので sounds softer than から (kara; VI-3) and is therefore often used when politeness is called for. When more politeness is required, there is recourse to もので (mono de; VI-5). ので is similar to て (-te; VI-1) in that they can both connect clauses, but ので has a softer sound. English equivalents: "because," "in that."

i) 今年の夏休みは、悪性の風邪が流行した**ので**、海外旅行者が激減した。
Kotoshi no natsu-yasumi wa, akusei no kaze ga ryūkō shita **no de**, kaigai-ryokōsha ga gekigen shita.
During summer vacation this year, there was a bad cold going around, so there was a huge drop in travelers going abroad.

ii) 今は景気が上向きな**ので**、会社の経営もうまくいっているようだ。
Ima wa keiki ga uwamuki na **no de**, kaisha no keiei mo umaku itte iru yō da.
Now, with the economic upturn, the company is apparently doing well.

5. もので (mono de). In that it indicates a cause or reason at the end of a clause and follows verbs, adverbs, and adjectives, もので is similar to, and interchangeable with, ので (no de; VI-4); it differs from ので in that it has a more polite sound to it. English equivalents: "because," "in that," "for the reason that."

i) 昨日は子供が熱を出した**もので**、コンサートにご一緒
   できず、申し訳ございませんでした。
   Kinō wa kodomo ga netsu o dashita **mono de**, konsāto ni
   goissho dekizu, mōshiwake gozaimasen deshita.
   Yesterday my son/daughter had a fever, so that I wasn't able to
   accompany you to the concert. I offer my apologies.

ii) 山下：すみません。会議が長引いている**もので**、6時
       までにはそちらに伺えないのですが…
    野本：いいですよ。お待ちしていますから、気にしな
       いでください。

   Yamashita: Sumimasen. Kaigi ga nagabiite iru **mono de**, rokuji
   made ni wa sochira ni ukagaenai no desu ga …
   Nomoto: Ii desu yo. Omachi shite imasu kara, ki ni shinai de
   kudasai.

   Yamashita: I'm very sorry, but the meeting has taken longer than
   expected and so I won't be able to call on you by 6 o'clock.
   Nomoto: That's perfectly all right. I'll be waiting for you, so don't
   concern yourself about it.

QUIZ VI

QUIZ VI–1

Choose the correct particle from among those following the sample sentences. Answers are at the end of the quiz, along with English translations.

1. とてもきれいだ（　　）この 花を買って帰りましょう。
   Totemo kirei da (　　) kono hana o katte kaerimashō.

   1. ので (no de)　2. から (kara)　3. て (-te)　4. もので (mono de)

2. 面白い（　　）もう一度この映画を見たい。
   Omoshiroi (　　) mō ichido kono eiga o mitai.

   1. ので (no de)　2. て (-te)　3. だから (da kara)　4. なので (na no de)

3. 昨晩はなんだか眠く（　　）、全然勉強ができなかった。
   Sakuban wa nan da ka nemuku (　　), zenzen benkyō ga dekinakatta.

   1. から (kara)　2. ので (no de)　3. て (-te)　4. もので (mono de)

4. 外は吹雪（　　）、今夜は出かけない方がいい。
   Soto wa fubuki (　　), konya wa dekakenai hō ga ii.

   1. なので (na no de)　2. から (kara)　3. もので (mono de)　4. て (-te)

5. この商品は高価（　　）、気をつけて扱ってくださいね。
   Kono shōhin wa kōka (　　), ki o tsukete atsukatte kudasai ne.

   1. ので (no de)　2. だから (da kara)　3. て (-te)　4. で (de)

6. この2、3日、体の調子が悪い（　　）、申し訳ないのですが、明日の食事の約束を来週に延ばして頂きたいと思います。

   Kono ni-san-nichi, karada no chōshi ga warui (　　), mōshiwake nai no desu ga, ashita no shokuji no yakusoku o raishū ni nobashite itadakitai to omoimasu.

   1. て (-te)　2. なので (na no de)　3. で (de)　4. もので (mono de)

7. 温泉に行ったのに、お湯が熱く（　　）、入れなかった。
   Onsen ni itta no ni, oyu ga atsuku (　　), hairenakatta.

   1. から (kara)　2. ので (no de)　3. て (-te)　4. もので (mono de)

8. あのハンドバッグが欲しかったが、とても高かった（　　）買えなかった。
   Ano handobaggu ga hoshikatta ga, totemo takakatta (　　) kaenakatta.

   1. ので (no de)　2. だから (da kara)　3. で (de)　4. なので (na no de)

9. 飛行機事故（　　）、空港は今閉鎖しているそうです。
   Hikōki-jiko (　　), kūkō wa ima heisa shite iru sō desu.

   1. から (kara)　2. で (de)　3. ので (no de)　4. もので (mono de)

10. 地球温暖化（　　）、世界の天気が変わってきているそうだ。
    Chikyū-ondanka (　　), sekai no tenki ga kawatte kite iru sō da.

    1. ので (no de)　2. から (kara)　3. もので (mono de)　4. で (de)

Answers and Translations for Quiz VI–1

1 = 2. Since they're so pretty, I'll just buy some of these flowers (and go home).
2 = 1. Since this movie is so interesting, I'd like to see it again.
3 = 3. For some reason I was so sleepy last night, I couldn't study at all.
4 = 1. Since there's a snowstorm outside, we'd better not go out tonight.
5 = 2. Since this product is terribly expensive, please handle it with care.
6 = 4. In that I have not been feeling well these last two or three days, I hate to ask, but I would like to postpone tomorrow's dinner engagement until next week.
7 = 3. Although I went to a hot spring, the water was so hot I couldn't get in.
8 = 1. I wanted that handbag, but it was so expensive I couldn't buy it.
9 = 2. Because of an airplane accident, the airport is said to be closed now.
10 = 4. Because of global warming, the world's climate is said to be changing.

QUIZ VI–2

Choose the correct particle from among those given in parentheses. Answers are at the end of the quiz, along with English translations.

1. 2年前の戦争 (から ｜ で) 大勢の人々が死んだ。
   Ninen mae no sensō (kara ｜ de) ōzei no hitobito ga shinda.

2. 昨日は暑く (て ｜ で)、冷たいものばかり飲んでいた。
   Kinō wa atsuku (-te ｜ de), tsumetai mono bakari nonde ita.

3. この本は字が小さい (ので ｜ て)、目が疲れる。
   Kono hon wa ji ga chiisai (no de ｜ -te), me ga tsukareru.

4. おそくなると寒くなる (から ｜ ものので)、急いで帰ろう。
   Osoku naru to samuku naru (kara ｜ mono de), isoide kaerō.

5. これは面白い映画 (だので ｜ なので)、ぜひ見てください。
   Kore wa omoshiroi eiga (da no de ｜ na no de), zehi mite kudasai.

6. この地方は、冬は雪が多い (だから ｜ から)、住むのはなかなか大変だ。

Kono chihō wa, fuyu wa yuki ga ōi (da kara | kara), sumu no wa nakanaka taihen da.

7. 山本さんは、声がきれい（ので｜なので）、歌手になれるかもしれない。
   Yamamoto-san wa, koe ga kirei (no de | na no de), kashu ni nareru ka mo shirenai.

8. 母：料理作ってるんだけど、ちょっと手伝ってくれない？
   娘：今友達にメールしてる（なので｜から）、終わるまで待って。
   Haha: Ryōri tsukutte 'ru n' da kedo, chotto tetsudatte kurenai?
   Musume: Ima tomodachi ni mēru shite 'ru (na no de | kara), owaru made matte.

9. あのレストランは、おいしく（から｜て）安いから、よく行きます。
   Ano resutoran wa, oishiku (kara | -te) yasui kara, yoku ikimasu.

10. 猛：空を見てごらん、きれいだから。
    緑：まぶしく（ので｜て）、目が開けられないの。
    Takeshi: Sora o mite goran, kirei da kara.
    Midori: Mabushiku (no de | -te), me ga akerarenai no.

Answers and Translations for Quiz VI-2

1 = で (de). Many people died in the war two years ago.
2 = て (-te). Yesterday it was so hot I was drinking nothing but cold drinks.
3 = ので (no de). The type in this book is so small, my eyes get tired.
4 = から (kara). It'll get cold later in the day, so let's hurry home.
5 = なので (na no de). This is an interesting movie, so you should definitely see it.
6 = から (kara). There is a lot of snow in this region, so living here is not all that easy.
7 = なので (na no de). Yamamoto-san has such a pretty voice, maybe she can become a singer.
8 = から (kara). Mother: I'm preparing something to eat. Could you give me a hand? Daughter: I'm emailing a friend right now, so wait till I finish.
9 = て (-te). The food at that restaurant is good and inexpensive, so I often go there.
10 = て (-te). Takeshi: Look at the sky. It's so pretty. Midori: I can't open my eyes because of the glare.

VII

Particles that Indicate a Condition or Supposition

1. ば (-ba)
2. たら (-tara)
3. なら (nara)
4. ところで (tokoro de)
5. ても、でも (-te mo, -de mo)
6. と (to)

> The particles in this group often overlap, and it is beyond the scope of this book to detail the multitudinous examples of overlapping. I will, instead, try to point out their core usages.

1. ば (-ba). Indicates a condition ("providing that...," "on the condition that ...") at the end of a clause, which is followed by another clause telling what will happen if the condition is, or were, true. The second clause cannot express an intention, desire, command, or request, though there are exceptions to this rule. The clause or sentence in which ば appears is often preceded by the word もし (moshi, if). English equivalent: "if."

i) 経済が安定していれば、この問題は解決できる。
 Keizai ga antei shite ire**ba**, kono mondai wa kaiketsu dekiru.
 If the economy were stable, this problem could be resolved.

ii) あまり高ければ、今回はあきらめよう。
 Amari takakere**ba**, konkai wa akirameyō.
 If it's too expensive, let's pass on it this time.

71

2. たら (-tara). Indicates a supposition ("supposing that," "if ... should happen"). It is different from ば (-ba; VII-1) in that it is more typical of the spoken language and can be used to express intentions, desires, commands, or requests without limitation. It can be preceded by the word もし (moshi; if) to emphasize the suppositional nature of たら. English equivalent: "if."

> i) もし明日雨が降っ**たら**、テニスには行かないつもりです。
> Moshi ashita ame ga fut**tara**, tenisu ni wa ikanai tsumori desu.
> If it rains tomorrow, I don't plan to go and play tennis.

> ii) 志乃：今、自由に使えるお金があっ**たら**、何がしたい？
> 幸子：そうね、船で外国旅行に行きたい。
>
> Shino: Ima, jiyū ni tsukaeru okane ga at**tara**, nani ga shitai?
> Sachiko: Sō ne, fune de gaikoku-ryokō ni ikitai.
>
> Shino: If you had some money right now that you could use in any way you wanted, what would you want to do?
> Sachiko: Well, yes, I'd like to go abroad by boat.

3. なら (nara). Indicates supposition like ば (-ba; VII-1) and たら (-tara; VII-2), but it often lays emphasis on the word preceding it (and might be translated "only if"). If the word preceding なら has already been previously mentioned, there is often some reason for suspecting that the supposition is true. English equivalent: "if."

> i) あの人**なら**、この仕事を引き受けてくれるでしょう。
> Ano hito **nara**, kono shigoto o hikiukete kureru deshō.
> If it's him (that you are talking about/who is being considered), he will surely take on this job. / He, if anyone, will take on this job for us.

> ii) そんなに行きたい**なら**、行ったらいい。

Sonna ni ikitai **nara**, ittara ii.
If you want to go that badly, go ahead and go.

4. ところで (tokoro de). Indicates a condition, with the connotation that even if the condition is met, the results will not be favorable. It is followed by a verb in the negative form. It is similar to ても (-te mo; VII-5) in presenting a condition that is not likely to meet with favorable results and being followed by a negative verb, but ところで is the more emphatic and preceded by a verb in the plain past form. English equivalent: "even if."

i) 今から車で行った**ところで**、3時の新幹線にはとても間に合わないよ。
Ima kara kuruma de itta **tokoro de**, sanji no shinkansen ni wa totemo ma ni awanai yo.
Even if you leave now by car, you're not going to make the 3:00 Bullet train.

ii) あの人に説明してみた**ところで**、わかってはくれないだろう。
Ano hito ni setsumei shite mita **tokoro de**, wakatte wa kurenai darō.
Even if you try explaining it to him, he's not going to understand you.

5. ても、でも (-te mo, -de mo). Indicates a supposition with verbs, adjectives, and nouns, with the understanding that even if the supposition were true, the results would not be good or meet expectations. It consists of the て (-te) form of a verb plus も (mo) or でも following nouns and na-adjective. English equivalent: "even if."

i) あなたが行っ**ても**、私は行かないつもりです。
Anata ga it**te mo**, watashi wa ikanai tsumori desu.
Even though you go, I don't intend to.

ii) お金がなくても、幸せになれると思います。
　　Okane ga naku**te mo**, shiawase ni nareru to omoimasu.
　　Even without money, I think it's possible to be happy.

6. と (to). Indicates a condition, as do ば (ba; VII-1), たら (-tara; VII-2), and なら (nara; VII-3), but it can also indicate that if a condition is met, the result will invariably follow, and for that reason it is sometimes translated as "when." Further, と is not used to express intention, commands, questions, requests, desires, and in that respect is similar to ば. English equivalent: "if," "when."

i) お酒を飲み過ぎると、頭が痛くなる。
　　Osake o nomisugiru **to**, atama ga itaku naru.
　　If (when) I drink too much alcohol, I get a headache.

ii) あまり高いと、あの人は買わないと思いますよ。
　　Amari takai **to**, ano hito wa kawanai to omoimasu yo.
　　If it is too expensive, I don't think that person (i.e., he or she) will buy it.

iii) 家に帰るまで、雨が降らないといいですね。
　　Ie ni kaeru made, ame ga furanai **to** ii desu ne.
　　It'd be nice, wouldn't it, if it didn't rain until we got home.

QUIZ VII

QUIZ VII–1

After reading the English translation, write in the parentheses the word that completes the Japanese sample sentences. An English translation is provided as a hint. For some of the sentences, there is more than one correct answer. Answers are at the end of the quiz.

1. If the weather is good tomorrow, shall we go for a drive?
   明日天気が（　　）ドライブに行きませんか？
   Ashita tenki ga (　　) doraibu ni ikimasen ka?

2. Even some Japanese can't read kanji at this level.
   日本人（　　）このくらいの漢字が読めない人もいます。
   Nihon-jin (　　) kono kurai no kanji ga yomenai hito mo imasu.

3. If the movie is that interesting, I want to see it too.
   そんなに面白い映画（　　）私も観たい。
   Sonna ni omoshiroi eiga (　　) watashi mo mitai.

4. No matter how hard I try, I can't possibly finish it.
   いくら努力した（　　）、私にはとても完成できない。
   Ikura doryoku shita (　　), watashi ni wa totemo kansei dekinai.

5. If it's all right with you, please come to my home this week for a visit.
   もし（　　）週末私の家へ遊びにいらっしゃいませんか？

Moshi (　　) shūmatsu watashi no uchi e asobi ni irasshaimasen ka?

Answers for Quiz VII-1

1 = よければ／よかったら (yokereba/yokattara).
2 = でも (-de mo).
3 = なら／だったら (nara/dattara).
4 = ところで (tokoro de).
5 = よければ／よろしければ (yokereba/yoroshikereba).

QUIZ VII-2

Conjugate the words in parentheses into their proper forms.

EXAMPLE
あなたが (行く ► 行けば) 私も行きます。
Anata ga (iku ► ikeba) watashi mo ikimasu.

1. 地震が (来る ►　　) どこへ逃げればいいんでしょうか？
   Jishin ga (kuru ►　　) doko e nigereba ii n' deshō ka?

2. 休みが (とれる ►　　) 海外旅行に出かけたいと思っています。
   Yasumi ga (toreru ►　　) kaigai-ryokō ni dekaketai to omotte imasu.

3. 明日は日曜日だから、天気が（よい ▶　　　）公園に来る人が多いだろう。
   Ashita wa nichiyōbi da kara, tenki ga (yoi ▶　　　) kōen ni kuru hito ga ōi darō.

4. 明日ひま（だ ▶　　　）、映画を観に行きませんか？
   Ashita hima (da ▶　　　), eiga o mi ni ikimasen ka?

5. 山田さんに（頼む ▶　　　）やってくれますよ。
   Yamada-san ni (tanomu ▶　　　) yatte kuremasu yo.

6. 京都へ（行く ▶　　　）、そのお寺の写真をたくさん撮るつもりです。
   Kyōto e (iku ▶　　　), sono otera no shashin o takusan toru tsumori desu.

7. 雪が（降り始める ▶　　　）すぐ家に帰ってこなければだめよ。
   Yuki ga (furihajimeru ▶　　　) sugu ie ni kaette konakereba dame yo.

8. 月給が（上がる ▶　　　）、新しいマンションに引っ越すつもりです。
   Gekkyū ga (agaru ▶　　　), atarashii manshon ni hikkosu tsumori desu.

9. 竹本さんが（来ない ▶　　　）、会議が始められないよ。
   Takemoto-san ga (konai ▶　　　), kaigi ga hajimerarenai yo.

10. 交通渋滞（だ ▶　　　）1時間で空港まで行くのは無理でしょう。
    Kōtsū-jūtai (da ▶　　　) ichi-jikan de kūkō made iku no wa muri deshō.

QUIZ VII

Answers and Translations for Quiz VII-2

1 = 来たら (kitara). If there is an earthquake, where should we take refuge?
2 = とれたら (toretara). If I can take some days off, I'd like to leave for a trip abroad.
3 = よかったら／いいなら (yokattara/ii nara) or よければ (yokereba) or よいと／いいと (yoi to/ii to) or よいなら (yoi nara). Since tomorrow is a Sunday, there will probably be a lot of people coming to the park if the weather is fine.
4 = だったら (dattara) or なら (nara). If you are free tomorrow, how about going to see a movie?
5 = 頼めば (tanomeba) or 頼んだら (tanondara) or 頼むと (tanomu to). If you ask Yamada-san, she do it for you.
6 = 行ったら (ittara). If I go to Kyoto, I plan to take a lot of pictures of that temple.
7 = 降り始めたら (furihajimetara). If it starts snowing, you've got to come home right away.
8 = 上がったら (agattara). If I get a raise in salary, I plan to move to a new condominium.
9 = 来ないと (konai to) or 来なかったら (konakattara) or 来なければ (konakereba) or 来ないなら (konai nara). We can't start the meeting if Takemoto-san doesn't show up.
10 = だったら (dattara) or なら (nara) or だと (da to). If it's congested, there is no way you can get to the airport in an hour.

Particles that Indicate a Limitation or Maximum

1. しか (shika)
2. だけ (dake)
3. だけしか (dake shika)
4. のみ (nomi)
5. きり (kiri)
6. きりしか (kiri shika)
7. のみしか (nomi shika)

🖉 The particles here are very similar to those give in group XV, and the sample sentences given in that group should be compared to those given here for better understanding.

1. しか (shika). Indicates a single instance or small amount of something and is followed by a verb in the negative form (unlike だけ [dake; VIII-2], which is followed by an affirmative verb.) English equivalent, "only."

i) 橋本：今日の飲み会、何人来るの？
河田：みんな忙しくて、5人しか来ないよ。

Hashimoto: Kyō no nomikai, nannin kuru no?
Kawada: Minna isogashikute, gonin **shika** konai yo.

Hashimoto: How many are coming to the drinking party today?
Kawada: Everyone's busy, so only five are coming.

ii) 昨日は3時間しか寝られなかったので、今日は寝不足だ。
Kinō wa sanji-kan **shika** nerarenakatta no de, kyō wa nebusoku da.

I only got three hours of sleep yesterday, so I feel drowsy today.

2. だけ (dake). Like しか (shika; VIII-1), indicates a single instance or small amount of something, but it differs in that is is followed by an affirmative verb. English equivalent: "only."

> i) 電話で簡単な報告**だけ**は聞いたが、まだ詳しいことはよくわからない。
> Denwa de kantan na hōkoku **dake** wa kiita ga, mada kuwashii koto wa yoku wakaranai.
> I got only a brief report over the phone, and I don't really know the details yet.
>
> ii) その事故で助かった人は、3人**だけ**でした。
> Sono jiko de tasukatta hito wa, sannin **dake** deshita.
> There were only three people rescued in that accident.

3. だけしか (dake shika). Like だけ (dake; VIII-2) and しか (shika; VIII-3), indicates a single instance or a small amount, but it is more emphatic than either. It is followed by a verb in the negative form. English equivalent: "only," "just."

> i) この映画は、1週間**だけしか**上映されない。
> Kono eiga wa, isshūkan **dake shika** jōei sarenai.
> This movie is showing for just one week.
>
> ii) ひろみ：雪はフランスには何回も行ったんでしょう？
> 雪：ううん、フランスはこれまで、1回**だけしか**行ってないわよ。
> Hiromi: Yuki wa Furansu ni wa nankai mo itta n' deshō?
> Yuki: Uun, Furansu wa kore made, ikkai **dake shika** itte 'nai wa yo.
> Hiromi: Yuki, you've gone to France any number of times, right?
> Yuki: Uh-uh, up to now I've been to France just once.

4. のみ (nomi). Like だけ (dake; VIII-2), indicates a single instance or a small amount and is followed by an affirmative verb, but differs in that it is more formal and characteristic of the written language. English equivalent: "only."

i) このカタログには、作者の初期の作品**のみ**記されている。
Kono katarogu ni wa, sakusha no shoki no sakuhin **nomi** shirusarete iru.
Only the early works of artists are recorded in this catalog.

ii) この保険は、資格審査に合格した者**のみ**加入できる。
Kono hoken wa, shikaku-shinsa ni gōkaku shita mono **nomi** ka'nyū dekiru.
This insurance is open only to those who have passed the qualifying examination. / Only those who have passed the qualifying exam can get this insurance.

5. きり (kiri). Like だけ (dake; VIII-2), indicates a single instance or a small amount, but is more characteristic of the spoken language. English equivalent: "just."

i) 彼は1か月前にここに来た**きり**、その後は全く現れない。
Kare wa ikkagetsu mae ni koko ni kita **kiri**, sono ato wa mattaku arawarenai.
He came here just once a month ago, and hasn't showed up at all since then.

ii) 子供：もう一つチョコレート、食べてもいい？
母：そんなに甘い物を食べると虫歯になるわよ。あと一つ**きり**よ。

Kodomo: Mō hitotsu chokorēto, tabete mo ii?
Haha: Sonna ni amai mono o taberu to mushiba ni naru wa yo. Ato hitotsu **kiri** yo.

Child: Can I have one more piece of chocolate?
Mother: Keep eating sweet things like that and your teeth will rot. Just one more and that's it.

6. きりしか (kiri shika). Identical to きり (kiri; VIII-5) in that it indicates a single instance or small amount, and is typical of the spoken language, but different in that it is more emphatic and is followed by a negative verb, as is しか (shika; VIII-1) when used alone. English equivalent: "only."

i) この商品は評判がよくて、もう一つ**きりしか**残っていません。
Kono shōhin wa hyōban ga yokute, mō hitotsu **kiri shika** nokotte imasen.
This product has such a good reputation, there is only one single item left.

ii) 夫：ビール、ある？
妻：冷蔵庫の中よ。
夫：もう1本**きりしか**ないよ。

Otto: Bīru, aru?
Tsuma: Reizōko no naka yo.
Otto: Mō ippon **kiri shika** nai yo.

Husband: Is there any beer?
Wife: In the frig.
Husband: There's only one bottle left.

7. のみしか (nomi shika). Indicates a single instance or a small amount, but because of しか (shika; VIII-1), it is more emphatic than のみ (nomi; VIII-4) alone and takes a negative verb; it is more formal than だけしか (dake shika; VIII-3) and きりしか (kiri shika; VIII-6). English equivalent: "only."

i) 今年の夏は天候不順で、収穫は例年の3分の1**のみし
かなかった。**
Kotoshi no natsu wa tenkō-fujun de, shūkaku wa reinen no sanbun no ichi **nomi shika** nakatta.
Because of the changeable summer weather this year, the harvest amounted to only one-third of the norm.

ii) この本には、大正時代の問題**のみしか**論じられていない。
Kono hon ni wa, taishō jidai no mondai **nomi shika** ronjirarete inai.
Only issues concerning the Taisho Period are discussed in this book.

QUIZ VIII

QUIZ VIII–1

Choose the correct particle from among those given below the sample sentences. Answers are at the end of the quiz, along with English translations.

1. 橋田：毎日、ジョギングしてるんだって？
   松山：うん、してるといっても30分（　　）だけどね。
   Hashida: Mainichi, jogingu shite 'ru n' datte?
   Matsuyama: Un, shite 'ru to itte mo sanjuppun (　　) da kedo ne.

   1. しか (shika)　2. だけ (dake)　3. だけしか (dake shika)　4. きりしか (kiri shika)

2. 真紀子：もうあの本読んだ？
   花江：まだ1ページ（　　）読んでないの。
   Makiko: Mō ano hon yonda?
   Hanae: Mada ippēji (　　) yonde 'nai no.

   1. しか (shika)　2. だけ (dake)　3. のみ (nomi)　4. しかだけ (shika dake)

3. 由美：きれいな花ね。この花、1年に何回も咲くの？
   ゆり：そんなに咲かないわよ。1年に1回（　　）よ。
   Yumi: Kirei na hana ne. Kono hana, ichinen ni nankai mo saku no?
   Yuri: Sonna ni sakanai wa yo. Ichinen ni ikkai (　　) yo.

   1. だけしか (dake shika)　2. のみしか (nomi shika)　3. だけ (dake)　4. しか (shika)

4. 竹内：今度の飛行機事故、こわかったですね。
   依田：そう、生存者はたった3人（　　）だったそうですね。
   Takeuchi: Kondo no hikōki-jiko, kowakatta desu ne.
   Yoda: Sō, seizonsha wa tatta sannin (　　) datta sō desu ne.

   1. しか (shika)　2. だけしか (dake shika)　3. のみ (nomi)　4. のみしか (nomi shika)

5. 母：もうご飯食べたの？駄目じゃない、肉（　　）食べてないわ。野菜も食べなきゃ大きくなれないわよ。
   息子：だって、にんじん嫌いなんだもん。
   Haha: Mō gohan tabeta no? Dame ja nai, niku (　　) tabete 'nai wa. Yasai mo tabenakya ōkiku narenai wa yo.
   Musuko: Datte, ninjin kirai nan da mon.

   1. だけ (dake)　2. のみ (nomi)　3. しか (shika)　4. だけのみ (dake nomi)

Answers and Translations for Quiz VIII-1

1 = 2. Hashida: So you go jogging every day, I hear. Matsuyama: Yeah, you could say that, but it's only for 30 minutes.
2 = 1. Makiko: Did you already read that book? Hanae: So far I've only read one page.
3 = 3. Yumi: Such a pretty flower. Does it blossom many times a year? Yuri: It doesn't blossom all that much. Only once a year.
4 = 3. Takeuchi: The airplane crash this time, that was really scary. Yoda: Yes, and I hear there were only three survivors.
5 = 3. Mother: Have you already eaten? That won't do, eating only the meat. If you don't eat your vegetables, you won't grow up big and strong. Son: But I hate carrots.

QUIZ VIII–2

Choose the correct particle from among those given in parentheses. Answers are to be found at the end of the quiz, along with English translations.

1. 川村：昨晩は寒くて、雪がかなり降りましたね。
   山下：ええ、でも2センチぐらい（しか｜のみ）積もりませんでしたよ。
   Kawamura: Sakuban wa samukute, yuki ga kanari furimashita ne.
   Yamashita: Ee, demo ni-senchi gurai (shika | nomi) tsumorimasen deshita yo.

2. 高橋：あの国に行くときは、ビザも必要でしょうね。
   小山：いいえ、パスポート（だけ｜しか）あれば、大丈夫らしいですよ。
   Takahashi: Ano kuni ni iku toki wa, biza mo hitsuyō deshō ne.
   Koyama: Iie, pasupōto (dake | shika) areba, daijōbu rashii desu yo.

3. 由香：デパートで今バーゲンやってるんだけど、行かない？
   亜紀：今日は5000円（より｜だけ）しかないんだけど、買える物あるかな。
   Yuka: Depāto de ima bāgen yatte 'ru n' da kedo, ikanai?
   Aki: Kyō wa gosen-en (yori | dake) shika nai n' da kedo, kaeru mono aru ka na.

4. 貴之：昨日、あれから飲みに行ったの？
   雅弘：行った、行った。でもビール2本飲んだ（しか｜だけ）だったけどね。
   Takayuki: Kinō, are kara nomi ni itta no?
   Masahiro: Itta, itta. Demo bīru nihon nonda (shika | dake) datta kedo ne.

5. 春美：新しいマンション、駅から随分遠いんでしょう？
   祐子：ううん、歩いても7、8分くらい（だけ｜しか）かからないの。
   Harumi: Atarashii manshon, eki kara zuibun tōi n' deshō?
   Yūko: Uun, aruite mo shichi-hachi-fun kurai (dake | shika) kakaranai no.

Answers and Translations for Quiz VIII-2

1. しか (shika). Kawamura: Last night was really cold, and there was a heavy snowfall. Yamashita: Right, but it amounted to only about 2 centimeters.
2. だけ (dake). Takahashi: When you go to that country, I wonder if you need a visa. Koyama: No, it seems that if you just have a passport, that's enough.
3. だけ (dake). Yuka: There is a bargain sale at the department store right now. Do you want to go? Aki: Today all I have is 5,000 yen. I wonder if there's anything I can buy with that?
4. だけ (dake). Takayuki: Yesterday, did you go out drinking after that? Masahiro: We sure did. But all I had to drink was a couple of bottles of beer.
5. しか (shika). Harumi: Your new condominium, it's pretty far from the station, isn't it? Yuko: Not really. It only takes seven or eight minutes on foot.

IX

Particles Indicating, or Providing Information about, the Subject of a Clause or Sentence

1a-c. は (wa)
2. が (ga)
3. で (de)
4. も (mo)
5. として (toshite)
6. には (ni wa)

✎ As seen below, the principal difference between は and が is that the former is a topic marker whereas the latter is a subject maker.

1a. は (wa). One of the principal functions of this particle is to mark a topic. A topic is the word about which the rest of the sentence provides information.

i) 肉は食べ過ぎると、体によくありません。
Niku **wa** tabesugiru to, karada ni yoku arimasen.
Eating too much meat is not good for your health.

1b. は (wa). Indicates the subject of a sentence when the subject is something that the speaker and the listener are both aware of, such as the sun and moon, themselves as speaker and listener, or something already mentioned in the conversation.

i) 太陽は東から出て、西に沈みます。
Taiyō **wa** higashi kara dete, nishi ni shizumimasu.
The sun rises in the east and sets in the west.

ii) 今晩の月**は**とてもきれいですね。
Konban no tsuki **wa** totemo kirei desu ne.
The moon tonight is really beautiful, isn't it.

iii) 笠原：私は、このプロジェクトを進めたいと思っておりますが、松木さん**は**どうお考えですか？
松木：私**は**、もう少し時間をおいてからの方がいいかと思っています。

Kasahara: Watashi **wa**, kono purojekuto o susumetai to omotte orimasu ga, Matsuki-san **wa** dō okangae desu ka?
Matsuki: Watashi **wa**, mō sukoshi jikan o oite kara no hō ga ii ka to omotte imasu.

Kasahara: I would like to proceed with this project. What do you think, Matsuki-san?
Matsuki: I think that maybe we should have a little more breathing room (before proceeding).

iv) この建物**は**、約100年前に建てられました。
Kono tatemono **wa**, yaku hyakunen-mae ni tateraremashita.
This building was erected approximately 100 years ago.

1c. は (wa). One of the most frequent uses of は is to create a contrast. Compare the following two samples (the first slightly contrived) and note how は replaces を (o) into order to sharpen the contrast between "meat" and "fish." (In both samples, 私は [watashi wa] would most likely remain unspoken since it would be taken for granted.)

i) 私は肉**を**食べません。魚**を**食べます。
Watashi wa niku **o** tabemasen. Sakana **o** tabemasu.
I don't eat meat. I eat fish.

ii) 私は肉**は**食べませんが、魚**は**食べます。
Watashi wa niku **wa** tabemasen ga, sakana **wa** tabemasu.
I don't eat meat, but I do eat fish.

2. が (ga). Indicates the subject of a clause or sentence, particularly when the speaker is mentioning a subject that the listener is hearing for the first time. This contrasts with は (wa; IX-1b), which marks a subject that the listener already knows about.

> i) その問題については、木村**が**担当していますので、木村に電話で問い合わせてください。
> Sono mondai ni tsuite wa, Kimura **ga** tantō shite imasu no de, Kimura ni denwa de toiawasete kudasai.
> Concerning that issue, Kimura is the person in charge, so please check with her.
>
> ii) 客：どのセーターがいいかしら？
> 店員：その白いの**が**、一番お似合いかと思いますが…
> Kyaku: Dono sētā ga ii kashira?
> Ten'in: Sono shiroi no **ga**, ichiban oniai ka to omoimasu ga ….
>
> Customer: I wonder which sweater would be best?
> Clerk: That white one would look best on you, I think.
>
> iii) 象は鼻**が**長い動物です。
> Zō wa hana **ga** nagai dōbutsu desu.
> Elephants are animals that have long noses.
>
>> ⌔ Here 象 (zō) is the subject of the sentence and 鼻 (hana) is the subject of 長い.
>
> iv) 花子さんは目**が**大きくて、かわいい。
> Hanko-san wa me **ga** ōkikute, kawaii.
> Hanako, with her big eyes, is cute.
>
>> ⌔ As seen below, following an interrogative (e.g., 誰 [dare; who], 何 [nani; what], どれ [dore; which], どこ [doko; where], どんな [donna; what kind]), が is always used, not は (wa), in asking a question. A straightforward answer also uses が after the subject.

i) 田中：どれ**が**あなたの傘ですか？
   渡辺：これ**が**私のです。

   Tanaka: Dore **ga** anata no kasa desu ka?
   Watanabe: Kore **ga** watashi no desu.

   Tanaka: Which is your umbrella?
   Watanabe: This one is mine.

ii) 記者：この会社では、どんな人材**が**必要なんですか？
    社長：まず、若い人**が**必要ですね。

   Kisha: Kono kaisha de wa, donna jinzai **ga** hitsuyō nan desu ka?
   Shachō: Mazu, wakai hito **ga** hitsuyō desu ne.

   Reporter: What kind of people/personnel are needed in this company?
   President: First of all, young people are needed.

⟡ As seen below, idiomatic expressions combining the verb する (suru; to do) with nouns such as 音 (oto; sound), 匂い (nioi; smell), 気持ち (kimochi; feeling), etc. ordinarily take が (ga) after the noun unless は (wa) is required for contrast or some other purpose.

i) コーヒーのいい匂い**が**する。
   Kōhī no ii nioi **ga** suru.
   There is the nice smell of coffee. / I can smell the aroma of coffee.

ii) 隣の部屋で、変な音**が**しました。
    Tonari no heya de, hen na oto **ga** shimashita.
    In the next room, there was a strange sound.

iii) 橘さんからその話を聞いて、いやな気持ち**が**した。
     Tachibana-san kara sono hanashi o kiite, iya na kimochi **ga** shita.

Hearing that story from Tachibana-san, I felt bad.

> As seen below, が is ordinarily used after the subjects of intransitive verbs, except when は (wa; IX-1) is required to create a contrast.

i) ここから富士山が見える。
Koko kara Fuji-san **ga** mieru.
Mt. Fuji can be seen from here.

ii) 電気が急に消えました。
Denki **ga** kyū ni kiemashita.
The electricity suddenly went off.

iii) 戸が開いた。
To **ga** aita.
The door opened.

> Compare the above with the following, which shows how は replaces が to create a contrast:

戸は開いたが、窓は開かなかった。
To **wa** aita ga, mado **wa** akanakatta.
The door opened, but the window didn't open.

3. で (de). Indicates how the subject carries out the action specified by the verb. The word preceding で often indicates how many people or what group carried out the action: e.g., 一人 (hitori; one person, oneself), みんな (minna; everyone), 家族 (kazoku; the family), or 委員会 (iinkai; committee). In the two samples given below, the subjects of the sentences are unspoken: in the first sample (first line), the subject is あなたは (anata wa; you) or the person's name; in the second it is うちは (uchi wa; my family) or 私たちは (watashi-tachi wa; we).

i) 朝子：今一人で住んでるの？
　美香子：そう、だから掃除も洗濯も、自分でしてる。

Asako: Ima hitori **de** sunde 'ru no?
Mikako: Sō, da kara sōji mo sentaku mo, jibun **de** shite 'ru.

Asako: You living by yourself now?
Mikako: Yeah, so I do both the cleaning and the laundry myself.

ii) 先週は、家族全員で温泉旅行に行ってきました。
Senshū wa, kazoku-zen'in **de** onsen-ryokō ni itte kimashita.
Last week the whole family went on a trip to a hot spring.

4. も (mo). Indicates the subject of a clause or sentence, replacing は (wa; IX-1) or が (ga; IX-2), and indicating that there is something else similar to the subject that has been mentioned previously. See also III-2–3, which look at も from a slightly different angle. English equivalent: "also," "too."

i) 青木君も、あの大学の試験を受けるとは、知らなかった。
Aoki-kun **mo**, ano daigaku no shiken o ukeru to wa, shiranakatta.
I didn't know that Aoki was also taking the exam to that university.

> ✎ In the above, the unspoken 私 (watashi) is the subject of the sentence. 青木君 (Aoki-kun) is the subject of the clause ending with 受ける (ukeru).

ii) あの評論家も、平和問題について論文を書いている。
Ano hyōron-ka **mo**, heiwa-mondai ni tsuite ronbun o kaite iru.
That critic is also writing a paper about the problem of peace.

5. として (toshite). Indicates the role or status in which the subject is functioning. English equivalent: "as."

i) あの体では、社長**として**働くのは無理ではないでしょうか？
Ano karada de wa, shachō **toshite** hataraku no wa muri de wa nai deshō ka?
With that body (being in that physical condition), isn't it impossible for him to work (function) as President?

> ✎ In the above, the subject of the sentence is unspoken. It could be, for example, Tanaka-san, the name of the President.

ii) 大学を卒業した今、皆さんは社会の一員**として**、これから頑張ってください。
Daigaku o sotsugyō shita ima, mina-san wa shakai no ichiin **toshite**, kore kara ganbatte kudasai.
Now that you have graduated from college, please do your utmost as a member of society.

6. には (ni wa). Indicates not the subject per se, but the person to whom a following judgment applies. English equivalent: "for."

i) 部長：山形君、明日から君に、新しい企画の責任者として、働いてもらいたいんだけど、どうかな？
山形：えっ、僕にですか？　そんな重大な仕事、僕**に****は**とても無理です。

Buchō: Yamagata-kun, ashita kara kimi ni, atarashii kikaku no sekininsha toshite, hataraite moraitai n' da kedo, dō ka na?
Yamagata: Ett, boku ni desu ka? Sonna jūdai na shigoto, boku **ni wa** totemo muri desu.

Department head: Yamagata, from tomorrow I want you to work as the responsible party (to take the responsibility) for the new project. What do you say?
Yamagata: What, me? A important job like that is quite beyond me.

ii) 姉：このブラウス、着てくれる？
    妹：いいけど、どうして？
    姉：私**には**、もう派手すぎるから…

Ane: Kono burausu, kite kureru?
Imōto: Ii kedo, dōshite?
Ane: Watashi **ni wa**, mō hadesugiru kara …

Older sister: Would you wear this blouse for me? / Do you want to wear this blouse?
Younger sister: Sure, but why?
Older sister: It's too flashy for me now.

QUIZ IX

QUIZ IX-1

Choose the correct particle from among those appearing below the sample sentences. Answers follow the quiz, along with English translations.

1. 山崎：これは僕の家族の写真です。
   美子：いいお写真ですね。どのかた（　　）お兄様ですか？
   Yamazaki: Kore wa boku no kazoku no shashin desu.
   Yoshiko: Ii oshashin desu ne. Dono kata (　　) onī-sama desu ka?

   1. は (wa)　2. も (mo)　3. が (ga)　4. として (toshite)

2. 私（　　）竹川と申します。どうぞよろしくお願いします。
   Watashi (　　) Takegawa to mōshimasu. Dōzo yoroshiku onegai shimasu.

   1. は (wa)　2. が (ga)　3. には (ni wa)　4. として (toshite)

3. 今日のパーティーには、泉田さんも、後藤さん（　　）来るはずです。
   Kyō no pātī ni wa, Izumida-san mo, Gotō-san (　　) kuru hazu desu.

   1. は (wa)　2. も (mo)　3. には (ni wa)　4. が (ga)

4. 石川：鈴木さんは、フランスに観光で行っていらしたんですか？
   鈴木：いいえ、政府の留学生（　　）行ったんですよ。
   Ishikawa: Suzuki-san wa, Furansu ni kankō de itte irashita n' desu ka?
   Suzuki: Iie, seifu no ryūgakusei (　　) itta n' desu yo.

   1. も (mo)　2. は (wa)　3. には (ni wa)　4. として (toshite)

5. 教授：細川さん、来月のゼミの発表をやってくれませんか？
   細川：えっ、私がですか？　このテーマ、私（　　）難しすぎて、無理です。
   Kyōju: Hosokawa-san, raigetsu no zemi no happyō o yatte kuremasen ka?
   Hosokawa: Ett, watashi ga desu ka? Kono tēma, watashi (　　) muzukashisugite, muri desu.

   1. は (wa)　2. も (mo)　3. には (ni wa)　4. が (ga)

Answers and Translations for Quiz IX-1

1 = 3. Yamazaki: This is a photo of my family. Yoshiko: What a lovely photo. Which one is your older brother?
2 = 1. My name is Takegawa. I am pleased to meet you.
3 = 2. Both Izumida-san and Goto-san should be coming to today's party.
4 = 4. Ishikawa: Did you go to France for sightseeing, Suzuki-san? Suzuki: No, I went as a government-sponsored exchange student.
5 = 3. Professor: Hosokawa-san, would you handle the report for the seminar next month? Hosokawa: What, me? This theme is much too difficult for me and simply out of the question.

QUIZ IX-2

Put the correct particle within the parentheses in the sample sentences. Answers follow the quiz, along with English translations.

1. 恵子：昨日彼と映画見に行ったんでしょう？
   友美：ううん、ゆりと二人（　　）行ったのよ。
   Keiko: Kinō kare to eiga mi ni itta n' deshō?
   Tomomi: Uun, Yuri to futari (　) itta no yo.

2. この大統領は、政治家というよりは音楽家（　　）有名だ。
   Kono daitōryō wa, seiji-ka to iu yori wa ongaku-ka (　　) yūmei da.

3. 今ニューヨークでは、どんなミュージカル（　　）面白いんですか？
   Ima Nyūyōku de wa, donna myūjikaru (　　) omoshiroi n' desu ka?

4. 松下教授（　　）今秋、英国の大学に研究に行かれるそうです。
   Matsushita kyōju (　　) konshū, Eikoku no daigaku ni kenkyū ni ikareru sō desu.

5. 小百合：明日のコンサート、何時からだった？
   かおる：6時からよ。ゆき（　　）来るんだって。
   Sayuri: Ashita no konsāto, nanji kara datta?
   Kaoru: Rokuji kara yo. Yuki (　) kuru n' datte.

Answers and Translations for Quiz IX-2

1 = で (de). Keiko: Yesterday you went to see a movie with your boyfriend, right? Tomomi: No, I went with Yuri.
2 = として (toshite). This President is more famous as a musician than as a politician.
3 = が (ga). What kind of musicals are interesting in New York now?
4 = は (wa). It is said that Professor Matsushita will be going to do research at a British university.
5 = も (mo). Sayuri: What time was tomorrow's concert from? Kaoru: Six o'clock. I hear Yuki is coming too.

X

Particles that Indicate Objects of Desire or Wishes

1. を (o)
2. が (ga)
3. に／へ (ni/e)

1. を (o). Indicates an object that is desired or wished for. を is commonly used with the たい (-tai) and たがる (-tagaru) forms of verbs. The former is used to refer to the speaker's wishes, and the latter to other people's; they cannot be interchanged. The たがる form often appears as たがっている (-tagatte iru). See also が (ga; X-2) for an explanation of how が can also be used with the たい form.

i) 今日はラーメンを食べたい。
Kyō wa rāmen **o** tabetai.
I want to eat ramen today.

ii) 子供は甘い物を食べたがります。
Kodomo wa amai mono **o** tabetagarimasu.
Children like to eat sweet things.

iii) 広岡さんは、新車を買いたがっています。
Hirooka-san wa, shinsha **o** kaitagatte imasu.
Hirooka-san wants to buy a new car.

2. が (ga). Indicates an object that is desired or wished for. It is commonly used with the adjective 欲しい (hoshii; to want), which can only refer to the speaker's wishes or wants. With 欲しい, が cannot be replaced by を. This is different from たい (-tai), which can take both が and を (o; X-1), with が being slightly more emphatic. 欲しい and たい can only be used in reference to the speaker's wishes or wants, not other people's.

    i) 私は、今新しいパソコン**が**欲しい。
       Watashi wa, ima atarashii pasokon **ga** hoshii.
       Right now I want a new PC.

    ii) 今日はラーメン**が**（を）食べたい。
       Kyō wa rāmen **ga** (o) tabetai.
       I want to eat ramen today.

3. に／へ (ni/e). Indicates a place to which one wishes to go when combined with verbs indicating desire, such as the たい (-tai) form, the たがる (-tagaru) form, and the adjective 欲しい (hoshii). This function is essentially the same as seen in IV-1. に and へ are interchangeable. English equivalent: "to."

    i) 夏休みには、海**に／へ**行きたい。
       Natsu-yasumi ni wa, umi **ni/e** ikitai.
       During summer vacation I want to go to the ocean.

    ii) 兄はこの夏、海外**に／へ**行きたがっている。
       Ani wa kono natsu, kaigai **ni/e** ikitagatte iru.
       My older brother is wanting to go abroad this summer.

    iii) 部長：来週、君に北海道の支店**に／へ**行ってほしいんだが、時間は大丈夫だろうか？
       Buchō: Raishū, kimi ni Hokkaidō no shiten **ni/e** itte hoshii n' da ga, jikan wa daijōbu darō ka?

Department head: I want you to go to the Hokkaido office next week. How are you fixed for time?

QUIZ X

QUIZ X-1

Choose the correct particle from the choices below the sample sentences. Answers follow the quiz, along with English translations.

1. この頃、若い人はあまり結婚(　　)したがりません。
   Kono goro, wakai hito wa amari kekkon (　　) shitagarimasen.

   1. ので (no de)　2. で (de)　3. を (o)　4. が (ga)

2. 今日は、辛い料理(　　)食べたい。
   Kyō wa, karai ryōri (　　) tabetai.

   1. が (ga)　2. と (to)　3. に (ni)　4. で (de)

3. 今年の夏は富士山(　　)登りたいと思っています。
   Kotoshi no natsu wa Fuji-san (　　) noboritai to omotte imasu.

   1. で (de)　2. に (ni)　3. と (to)　4. が (ga)

4. あまり高くなければ、新車(　　)買いたいんです。
   Amari takaku nakereba, shinsha (　　) kaitai n' desu.

   1. を (o)　2. で (de)　3. と (to)　4. や (ya)

5. その飛行機(　　)乗りたかったんです。
   Sono hikōki (　　) noritakatta n' desu.

   1. から (kara)　2. に (ni)　3. で (de)　4. が (ga)

Answers and Translations for Quiz X-1

1 = 3. These days young people don't want to marry very much.
2 = 1. I want to eat some spicy food today.
3 = 2. This summer I want to climb Mt. Fuji.
4 = 1. If it's not too expensive, I would like to buy a new car.
5 = 2. I wanted to embark on that plane (wanted to take that plane).

QUIZ X-2

Put the correct particle in the parentheses in each sample sentence. Answers follow the quiz, along with English translations.

1. 真奈美：どんな靴買うの？
   亜希子：色がきれいなの（　　　）欲しいの。
   Manami: Donna kutsu kau no?
   Akiko: Iro ga kirei na no (　　) hoshii no.

2. 昨日はゴルフ（　　）行きたかった。
   Kinō wa gorufu (　　) ikitakatta.

3. 週末、子供達はテレビゲーム（　　　）したがります。
   Shūmatsu, kodomo-tachi wa terebi-gēmu (　　) shitagarimasu.

4. 久しぶりでビール（　　）飲みたいね。
   Hisashiburi de bīru (　　) nomitai ne.

5. 来年は運転免許（　　）取りたいと思っています。
   Rainen wa unten-menkyo (　　) toritai to omotte imasu.

Answers and Translations for Quiz X-2

1 = が (ga). Manami: What kind of shoes are you going to buy? Akiko: I want something in a beautiful color.
2 = に (ni). I really wanted to play golf yesterday.
3 = を (o). On the weekends the children only want to play video games.
4 = が (ga) or を (o). Since it's been a while, I feel like having a beer.
5 = を (o) or が (ga). I am thinking about getting a driver's license next year.

XI

Particles that Indicate a List of Objects, Qualities, or Actions

1. や…や (ya … ya)
2. とか…とか (to ka … to ka)
3. だの…だの (dano… dano)
4. など (nado)
5. なんか (nanka)
6. に (ni)

🖎 See also Group III, which looks at some of these same particles from a different perspective.

1. や…や (ya … ya). Indicates a partial list of nouns that could be added to if the speaker wished to do so. In this respect, it is similar to とか…とか (to ka … to ka; XI-2) and だの…だの (dano … dano; XI-3), but both of these follow not only nouns but also adjectives and verbs. In contrast to や…や's standard way of presenting a partial list of nouns, とか…とか is more typical of the spoken language and presents concrete examples of a larger category. だの…だの, on the other hand, tends to present things that have a negative implication. English equivalent: "things such as … and …."

i) 松田：昨日の集まりに誰が来てた？
大山：矢田**や**、斉藤**や**、東野が来てたよ。

Matsuda: Kinō no atsumari ni dare ga kite 'ta?
Ōyama: Yada **ya**, Saitō **ya**, Higashino ga kite 'ta yo.

Matsuda: Who came to yesterday's gathering?
Oyama: Yada, Saito, Higashino came, among others.

ii) あの会社は、函館や、札幌や、根室に支店をもっている。
Ano kaisha wa, Hakodate **ya**, Sapporo **ya**, Nemuro ni shiten o motte iru.
That company has branches in Hakodate, Sapporo, Nemuro, and other places.

2. とか…とか (to ka ... to ka). Indicates concrete examples of what one is talking about. It follows nouns, adjectives, and verbs, distinguishing it from や…や (ya ... ya; XI-1), which follows nouns only. It is characteristic of spoken Japanese and does not necessarily have (but can have) the negative implications that だの…だの (dano ... dano; XI-3) tends to have. English equivalent: "and ... and ... and so on."

i) ゆみ：京都の天気よかった？
美子：そうね、小雨**とか**、曇り**とか**、天気は悪かったわ。

Yumi: Kyōto no tenki yokatta?
Yoshiko: Sō ne, kosame **to ka**, kumori **to ka**, tenki wa warukatta wa.

Yumi: Was the weather good in Kyoto?
Yoshiko: Well, there was a drizzle, it was cloudy, and so altogether it wasn't good.

ii) 佐々木：昨日のパーティー、どんな料理だった？
小山：いろいろあったわよ。お寿司**とか**、天ぷら**とか**、さしみ**とか**、唐揚げ**とか**、けっこうおいしかったわよ。

Sasaki: Kinō no pātī, donna ryōri datta?
Koyama: Iroiro atta wa yo. Osushi **to ka**, tenpura **to ka**, sashimi **to ka**, karaage **to ka**, kekkō oishikatta wa yo.

Sasaki: What kind of food was there at the party yesterday?
Koyama: There was all kinds of stuff. Sushi, tempura, sashimi, fried chicken, and stuff, and it was really pretty good.

✎ Among young Japanese, とか is often used to indicate a single example of what they are talking about rather than a list of things. It also may be used as a way to soften or lighten the request. In this usage, it is interchangeable with なんか (nanka; XI-5).

愛子：お茶**とか**飲む？
光：いいね、そうしよう。

Aiko: Ocha **to ka** nomu?
Hikaru: Ii ne, sō shiyō.

Aiko: Want to have tea or something?
Hikaru: Sounds good. Let's do it.

3. だの…だの (dano ... dano).
Indicates some examples of what one is talking about. It is characteristic of the spoken language and leaves the impression that the examples are somehow annoying or troublesome. It is similar to や…や (ya ... ya; XI-1) in that it can follow nouns and to とか…とか (to ka ... to ka; XI-2) in that it can follow adjectives, nouns, and verbs, but different in that neither of these necessarily leave a negative impression. English equivalent: "... and ... and other (annoying) things."

i) 母：また野菜食べてないじゃない。おいしくない**だの**、
　　　いや**だの**なんて言わないで、食べないと駄目よ。
　息子：食べるよ、いやだけど。

Haha: Mata yasai tabete 'nai ja nai. Oishiku nai **dano**, iya **dano** nante iwanai de, tabenai to dame yo.
Musuko: Taberu yo, iya da kedo.

Mother: You haven't eaten your vegetables again. Don't give me, "They don't taste good" or "I don't like them." You have to eat them.
Son: I'll eat them, but I don't want to.

ii) 不景気だの、倒産だの、リストラだの、いいニュースは一つもないですね。
Fukeiki dano, tōsan dano, risutora dano, ii nyūsu wa hitotsu mo nai desu ne.
Recession, bankruptcy, restructuring—there's not one bit of good news.

4. など (nado). Indicates that there are other things of the same nature as just presented. Often follows lists or examples given with や…や (ya ... ya; XI-1) and とか…とか (to ka ... to ka; XI-2) to emphasize the existence of other things that could be mentioned additionally. Like なんか (nanka; XI-5), it can also appear after a single word, not within a list, indicating that the word is to be taken as an example. English equivalent: "et cetera."

i) 郁子：ジョンって、いろんな言葉できるんですってね。
昭彦：そう、英語や、フランス語や、ドイツ語や、スペイン語や、ロシア語**など**もしゃべるらしいよ。

Ikuko: Jon tte, ironna kotoba dekiru n' desu tte ne.
Akihiko: Sō, Eigo ya, Furansugo ya, Doitsugo ya, Supeingo ya, Roshiago nado mo shaberu rashii yo.

Ikuko: John, you know, they say he speaks a lot of languages.
Akihiko: Apparently he can speak English, French, German, Spanish, Russian, and others besides.

ii) 鈴木：ヨーロッパでは、どんな国にいらっしゃいましたか？
高木：そうですね、フランスとか、イギリスとか、スイスとか、イタリアとか、オランダ**など**、いろいろな国に行ってみました。

Suzuki: Yōrroppa de wa, donna kuni ni irasshaimashita ka?
Takagi: Sō desu ne, Furansu to ka, Igirisu to ka, Suisu to ka, Itaria to ka, Oranda nado, iroiro na kuni ni itte mimashita.

Suzuki: Which countries did you visit in Europe?
Takagi: Let me see. I went to France, Britain, Switzerland, Italy, the Netherlands, and various countries.

iii) 酒井：お酒は何が好きですか？
　　清水：ジン**など**がいいですね。

Sakai: Osake wa nani ga suki desu ka?
Shimizu: Jin **nado** ga ii desu ne.

Sakai: What alcohol do you like?
Shimizu: Gin, say, is really nice.

5. なんか (nanka). Indicates that a list of words just presented is not complete, but that others could be added to it if the speaker wished to, or it follows a single word and indicates that that word, or thing, is the type of thing the speaker is talking about. なんか is a less polite form of など (nado; XI-4) and shares the above two functions with it. English equivalent: "for example," "say."

i) 美加：今日は何を食べましょうか？
　　知美：そうね、久しぶりで、ハンバーグ**なんか**どう？

Mika: Kyō wa nani o tabemashō ka?
Tomomi: Sō ne, hisashiburi de, hanbāgu **nanka** dō?

Mika: What shall we eat today?
Tomomi: Well, how about, say, hamburger for once in a great while?

ii) 後藤：この頃、太ってしまって、医者に何か運動するように、言われたんだけど、何がいいだろうかね。
　　酒井：そうですね。テニス**なんか**いいんじゃないですか？

Gotō: Kono goro, futotte shimatte, isha ni nanika undō suru yō ni, iwareta n' da kedo, nani ga ii darō ka ne.

Sakai: Sō desu ne. Tenisu **nanka** ii n' ja nai desu ka?

Goto: I have gained so much weight these days, I was told by the doctor to do some kind of exercise. I wonder what would be good.
Sakai: Let me see. Wouldn't, say, tennis be good?

6. に (ni). Indicates a complete list of nouns, except when followed by など (nado; et cetera; XI-4). It is more structured and typical of polite conversation than や…や (ya … ya; XI-1), とか…とか (to ka … to ka; XI-2), or だの…だの (dano … dano; XI-3), though close to the first of these three, and without the colloquialism of the second two and the negative implications of the third. English equivalent: "and," "with," "plus."

i) 日本の古い掛け軸の絵には、梅にうぐいす、竹に虎を描いたものが多いです。
Nihon no furui kakejiku no e ni wa, ume **ni** uguisu, take **ni** tora o egaita mono ga ōi desu.
In the paintings on old Japanese hanging scrolls, there is often a drawing of a plum tree with a bush warbler, or a tiger with bamboo.

ii) トム：日本ではお正月に、どんな食べ物を用意するんですか？
古川：家庭によって色々ですが、一般的には、年越しそばに、お雑煮に、おせち料理などですね。
Tomu: Nihon de wa oshōgatsu ni, donna tabemono o yōi suru n' desu ka?
Furukawa: Katei ni yotte iroiro desu ga, ippanteki ni wa, toshikoshi-soba **ni**, ozōni **ni**, osechi-ryōri nado desu ne.

Tom: What kind of food do you prepare in Japan for New Year's?
Furukawa: There is a lot of variation depending on the family, but generally speaking, there is food like New Year's noodles, a soup called *ozōni*, and special New Year's food called *osechi-ryōri*.

QUIZ XI

QUIZ XI–1

Choose the correct particle from within the parentheses below each sample sentence. Answers follow the quiz, along with English translations.

1. 直美：瑠実の誕生日のプレゼント、何がいいと思う？
   美智子：そうね、アクセサリー（　　）どうかしら。
   Naomi: Rumi no tanjōbi no purezento, nani ga ii to omou?
   Michiko: Sō ne, akusesarī (　　) dō kashira.

   1. や (ya)   2. に (ni)   3. なんか (nanka)

2. 昨日はデパートに行って、靴や、スカート（　　）、ベルトなどを買った。
   Kinō wa depāto ni itte, kutsu ya, sukāto (　　), beruto nado o katta.

   1. など (nado)   2. だの (dano)   3. や (ya)

3. あゆみ：来週のバス旅行に、誰が行くの？
   久子：はっきり行くって言ってるのは、山田さんに、藤田さん（　　）、日比野さんの、3人だけなのよ。
   Ayumi: Raishū no basu-ryokō ni, dare ga iku no?
   Hisako: Hakkiri iku tte itte 'ru no wa, Yamada-san ni, Fujita-san (　　), Hibino-san no, sannin dake na no yo.

   1. や (ya)   2. なんか (nanka)   3. に (ni)

4. 竹内：ジムさんの住んでいるハワイは、どんな果物がおいしいんですか？
   ジム：そうですね、マンゴーや、パパイヤや、パイナップル（　　）、いろいろありますよ。

   Takeuchi: Jimu-san no sunde iru Hawai wa, donna kudamono ga oishii n' desu ka?
   Jimu: Sō desu ne, mangō ya, papaiya ya, painappuru (　　), iroiro arimasu yo.

   1. だの (dano)　2. など (nado)　3. なんか (nanka)

5. 竹内：ジムさんは、どんな日本料理が好きですか？
   ジム：すき焼きとか、さしみ（　　）、すしとか、日本料理は何でも食べますよ。

   Takeuchi: Jimu-san wa, donna Nihon-ryōri ga suki desu ka?
   Jimu: Sukiyaki to ka, sashimi (　　), sushi to ka, Nihon-ryōri wa nandemo tabemasu yo.

   1. とか (to ka)　2. や (ya)　3. なんか (nanka)

Answers and Translations for Quiz XI-1

1 = 3. Naomi: What do you think is good for Rumi's birthday present? Michiko: How would, say, an accessory be?
2 = 3. Yesterday I went to a department store and bought shoes, a skirt, a belt, and some other things.
3 = 3. Ayumi: Who's going on the bus trip next week? Hisako: Those who say they are definitely going are Yamada-san, Fujita-san, and Hibino-san—just those three.
4 = 2. Takeuchi: In Hawaii, where you are living now, what fruit tastes really good? Jim: Well, there are mango, papaya, pineapple, et cetera—there are all kinds.
5 = 1. Takeuchi: What kind of Japanese cooking do you like, Jim? Jim: Sukiyaki, sashimi, and sushi—I'll eat any kind of Japanese food.

QUIZ XI–2

Insert the correct particle into the parentheses in the sample sentence. Answers follow the quiz, along with English translations.

1. まゆみ：幸の部屋、何が置いてあるの？
   幸：パソコンとか、テレビ（　　）、洋服ダンスとか、ベッドなんかあるわ。
   Mayumi: Sachi no heya, nani ga oite aru no?
   Sachi: Pasokon to ka, terebi (　　), yōfuku-dansu to ka, beddo nanka aru wa.

2. 客：サンドイッチはどんな種類があるんですか？
   ウエートレス：ハムサンドや、野菜サンド（　　）、フルーツサンドなどがございますが。
   Kyaku: Sandoitchi wa donna shurui ga aru n' desu ka?
   Uētoresu: Hamu-sando ya, yasai-sando (　　), furūtsu-sando nado ga gozaimasu ga.

3. 阿部：あなたの日本語のクラスには、どんな国の人がいるんですか？
   リー：そうですねえ、中国人（　　）、韓国人とか、オランダ人とか、ドイツ人とか、いろいろな国の人がいますよ。
   Abe: Anata no Nihongo no kurasu ni wa, donna kuni no hito ga iru n' desu ka?
   Rī: Sō desu ne, Chūgoku-jin (　　), Kankoku-jin to ka, Oranda-jin to ka, Doitsu-jin to ka, iroiro na kuni no hito ga imasu yo.

4. 京子：ハワイで、おいしい果物、食べた？
   光代：パイナップルだの、マンゴー（　　）、パパイヤだの、たくさん食べた。
   Kyōko: Hawai de, oishii kudamono, tabeta?
   Mitsuyo: Painappuru dano, mangō (　　), papaiya dano, takusan tabeta.

5. 高橋：明日の飲み会には、先生方も参加するんですか？
   井上：そうらしいんです。古川先生に、藤田先生（　　）、佐々木先生なんかもおいでになるらしいですよ。
   Takahashi: Ashita no nomikai ni wa, sensei-gata mo sanka suru n' desu ka?
   Inoue: Sō rashii n' desu. Furukawa sensei ni, Fujita sensei (　　), Sasaki sensei nanka mo oide ni naru rashii desu yo.

Answers and Translations for Quiz XI-2

1. とか (to ka). Mayumi: What do you have in your room, Sachi? Sachi: A PC, a TV, a chest of drawers, a bed, and stuff like that.
2. や (ya). Customer: What kind of sandwiches do you have? Waitress: To begin with, we have ham, vegetable, and fruit sandwiches.
3. とか (to ka). Abe: In your Japanese class, what countries are the students from? Lee: Let me see. There are people from all kinds of countries, like China, South Korea, the Netherlands, and Germany.
4. だの (dano). Kyoko: Did you eat some delicious fruit in Hawaii? Mitsuyo: I ate an awful lot, like pineapple, mango, and papaya.
5. に (ni). Takahashi: Are the teachers going to take part in the drinking party tomorrow? Inoue: It seems that way. Mr. Furukawa, Ms. Fujita, and Ms. Sasaki will be coming, for starters.

XII

Particles that Indicate an Amount or Quantity

1. くらい、ぐらい (kurai, gurai)
2. ほど (hodo)
3. ばかり、ばかし (bakari, bakashi)
4. ずつ (zutsu)
5. とも (tomo)
6. だけ (dake)
7. も (mo)

1. くらい、ぐらい (kurai, gurai). Indicates an approximate amount or quantity. The two variations have the same meaning and are largely interchangeable. Compared to ほど (hodo; XII-2) and ばかり、ばかし (bakari, bakashi; XII-3), this particle has the widest range in usage, both in terms of the kinds of words it can follow and in the situations in which it can be used. It has a slight tendency to point to the minimum of an approximate amount rather than the maximum. English equivalent: "about," "around."

i) 乗客：搭乗手続きが始まるまで、後何分**ぐらい**ありますか？
係員：後15分**くらい**でございますが。

Jōkyaku: Tōjō-tetsuzuki ga hajimaru made, ato nanpun **gurai** arimasu ka?
Kakari-in: Ato jūgo-fun **kurai** de gozaimasu ga.

Passenger: How much (how many minutes) longer will it be until the boarding procedures begin?
Attendant: It should be another 15 minutes or so.

ii) 妻：明日のお客様、何人**ぐらい**いらっしゃるの？
夫：6人来るよ。ビールを1ダースと、ワインを3本**ぐらい**、用意しておいて。

Tsuma: Ashita no okyaku-sama, nannin **gurai** irassharu no?
Otto: Rokunin kuru yo. Bīru o ichidāsu to, wain o sanbon **gurai**, yōi shite oite.

Wife: About how many guests will be coming tomorrow?
Husband: Six. Make sure we have a dozen beers and, say, three bottles of wine on hand.

2. ほど (hodo). Indicates an approximate amount or quantity with the connotation that it is the maximum that one might expect. It is a slightly more polite form, and more characteristic of the written language, than くらい、ぐらい (kurai, gurai; XII-1). These particles, plus ばかり (bakari; XII-3), can be used more out of a sense of politeness than accuracy, by making the amount somewhat vague (see example iii on the facing page). English equivalent: "approximately."

i) 古川：もしもし、井上課長をお願いします。
佐藤：ただいま席を外しております。あと10分**ほど**で、戻って参りますが。
古川：山本商事の古川と申しますが、20分**ほど**したら、もう一度お電話するとお伝えください。

Furukawa: Moshimoshi, Inoue kachō o onegai shimasu.
Satō: Tadaima seki o hazushite orimasu. Ato juppun **hodo** de, modotte mairimasu ga.
Furukawa: Yamamoto Shōji no Furukawa to mōshimasu ga, nijuppun **hodo** shitara, mō ichido odenwa suru to otsutae kudasai.

Furukawa: Hello. May I speak to Section Chief Inoue?
Sato: Mr. Inoue is not at his desk at the moment, but he should be back in about 10 minutes.

Furukawa: This is Mr. Furukawa at Yamamoto Shoji. Please tell Mr. Inoue that I will call again in about 20 minutes.

ii) 客：このパン、5個**ほど**欲しいんですが…
店員：申し訳ございません。もう2個しか残っておりませんが、後1時間**ほど**お待ち頂ければ、次のが焼きあがります。

Kyaku: Kono pan, go-ko **hodo** hoshii n' desu ga….
Ten'in: Mōshiwake gozaimasen. Mō ni-ko shika nokotte orimasen ga, ato ichi-jikan **hodo** omachi itadakereba, tsugi no ga yakiagarimasu.

Customer: I'd like, say, five of this kind of bread.
Clerk: I'm really sorry, but there are only two left. But if you can wait for an hour or so, we will finish baking the next batch.

iii) 銀行に行くのを忘れたので、1万円**ほど**貸してくれませんか？

Ginkō ni iku no o wasureta no de, ichiman-en **hodo** kashite kuremasen ka?

I forgot to go to the bank, and I wonder if you could lend me ten thousand yen or so.

3. ばかり、ばかし (bakari, bakashi). Indicates an approximate amount or quantity like くらい、ぐらい (kurai, gurai; XII-1) and ほど (hodo; XII-2), but focuses on the smallness of the amount. In this particular sense, ばかり has a slightly old-fashioned flavor, whereas ばかし is casual and used among friends and family. Since ばかり and ばかし focus on the smallness of the amount, they are not usually used with large figures. English equivalent: "approximately."

i) この仕事は2、3時間**ばかり**かかるでしょう。
Kono shigoto wa ni-san jikan **bakari** kakaru deshō.
This job will take approximately two or three hours.

ii) 疲れたので、2日**ばかし**旅行に行ってきた。
   Tsukareta no de, futsuka **bakashi** ryokō ni itte kita.
   I was tired, so I went off on a little trip for a couple of days.

4. ずつ (zutsu). Indicates that an amount or quantity is divided up equally into two or more parts. English equivalent: "each," "respectively."

i) こちらに、昨日の会議の議事録がおいてありますので、1部**ずつ**取ってください。
   Kochira ni, kinō no kaigi no gijiroku ga oite arimasu no de, ichibu-**zutsu** totte kudasai.
   The minutes of yesterday's meeting are right here. Please take one copy each.

ii) 1日に1万歩**ずつ**歩くと、健康にいいと言われています。
   Ichinichi ni ichimanpo-**zutsu** aruku to, kenkō ni ii to iwarete imasu.
   If you walk 10,000 steps a day, it is said to be good for your health.

5. とも (tomo). Indicates that all of the numbers specified are to be included, referring to two or more items. The meaning is "neither" or "none of" when followed by a negative verb. English equivalent: "both," "all of," "none of."

i) 宮本：川上さん、双子の赤ちゃんが生まれたそうですね。
   中島：そうですってね。二人**とも**女の子だそうですよ。

   Miyamoto: Kawakami-san, futago no akachan ga umareta sō desu ne.
   Nakajima: Sō desu tte ne. Futari **tomo** onna no ko da sō desu yo.

   Miyamoto: I hear that Kawakami-san has had twins.
   Nakajima: That's what I hear. They say that both are girls.

ii) えり：昨日セーター買ったんだって？
悦子：そう、2枚買ったんだけど、両方**とも**大きいの。

Eri: Kinō sētā katta n' datte?
Etsuko: Sō, ni-mai katta n' da kedo, ryōhō **tomo** ōkii no.

Eri: I hear you bought a sweater yesterday.
Etsuko: Uh-huh, I bought two, but they're both too big.

6. だけ (da**ke**). Indicates an amount or quantity that is an upper limit. The amount is usually small, though not necessarily so. English equivalent: "no more than," "only," "just."

i) 子供：アイスクリーム、買って。
母：一つ**だけ**よ。

Kodomo: Aisukurīmu, katte.
Haha: Hitotsu **dake** yo.

Child: Buy me some ice cream
Mother: But just one.

ii) ビールをコップ1杯**だけ**飲みました。
Bīru o koppu ippai **dake** nomimashita.
I had just one glass of beer.

7. も (mo). Indicates an amount or quantity that is an upper limit or a sufficient amount. It is often used with the ば (-ba; VII-1) form of a verb to indicate that a certain amount is sufficient under the conditions specified by ば. It is interchangeable with くらい、ぐらい (kurai, gurai; XII-1), ほど (hodo; XII-2), ばかり、ばかし (bakari, bakashi; XII-3), and だけ (dake; XII-6), though each has its own nuances. English equivalent: "as much as," "at most."

i) 山本：駅までどのくらいかかりますか？
平野：10分**も**あれば行けますよ。

Yamamoto: Eki made dono kurai kakarimasu ka?
Hirano: Juppun **mo** areba ikemasu yo.

Yamamoto: How long does it take to the station?
Hirano: You can get there within ten minutes.

ii) 私の部屋は狭いので、5人も入れば、いっぱいです。
Watashi no heya wa semai no de, go-nin **mo** haireba, ippai desu.

My room is so small that if you get as many as five people in it, it's full.

QUIZ XII

QUIZ XII–1

Choose the correct particle from those given below the sample sentence. Answers follow the quiz, along with English translations.

1. このコーヒーカップは、二つ（　　）フランス製です。
   Kono kōhī-kappu wa, futatsu (　) Furansu-sei desu.

   1. ぐらい (gurai)   2. ほど (hodo)   3. とも (tomo)

2. 子供達に、ケーキを1個（　　）配ってくれませんか？
   Kodomo-tachi ni, kēki o ikko (　) kubatte kuremasen ka?

   1. とも (tomo)   2. くらい (kurai)   3. ずつ (zutsu)

3. この仕事は、3時間（　　）あればできると思います。
   Kono shigoto wa, sanjikan (　) areba dekiru to omoimasu.

   1. ぐらい (gurai)   2. とも (tomo)   3. ずつ (zutsu)

4. 夫：もしもし、後10分（　　）したら、会社を出て帰るから。
   妻：はい、わかりました。
   Otto: Moshimoshi, ato juppun (　) shitara, kaisha o dete kaeru kara.
   Tsuma: Hai, wakarimashita.

   1. とも (tomo)   2. ほど (hodo)   3. ずつ (zutsu)

5. 絵里子：昨日のコンサート、どうだった？
   美紀：よかったんだけど、観客は50人（　　）でさびしかったわ。
   Eriko: Kinō no konsāto, dō datta?
   Miki: Yokatta n' da kedo, kankyaku wa gojū-nin (　　) de sabishikatta wa.

   1. ずつ (zutsu)　2. とも (tomo)　3. ばかり (bakari)

Answers and Translations for Quiz XII-1

1 = 3. These two coffee cups are both French-made.
2 = 3. Could you hand out one cake each to all the children?
3 = 1. Give us three hours or so, and I think we can finish this job.
4 = 2. Husband: Hi, I'll be leaving the office within ten minutes. Wife: Okay.
5 = 3. Eriko: How was the concert yesterday? Miki: It was okay, but the audience consisted of about fifty people, and so it was a little sad.

QUIZ XII-2

Insert the correct particle into the parentheses in the sample sentence. Answers are at the end of the quiz, along with English translations.

1. 福井：就職試験、二つ受けてたよね、どうだった？
   中島：それが、二つ（　　）駄目だったよ。
   Fukui: Shūshoku-shiken, futatsu ukete 'ta yo ne, dō datta?
   Nakajima: Sore ga, futatsu (　　) dame datta yo.

2. 泊まり客：夕食はルームサービスでお願いしたいんですけど、時間はどの（　　）かかりますか？
   ホテルの人：ご注文にもよりますが、30分ほどでお届けできます。

Tomari-kyaku: Yūshoku wa rūmu-sābisu de onegai shitai n' desu kedo, jikan wa dono (   ) kakarimasu ka?
Hoteru no hito: Gochūmon ni mo yorimasu ga, sanjuppun hodo de otodoke dekimasu.

3. 先生：今日の試験は2ページです。2ページ（   ）鉛筆で書いてください。
   生徒：わかりました。
   Sensei: Kyō no shiken wa ni-pēji desu. Ni-pēji (   ) enpitsu de kaite kudasai.
   Seito: Wakarimashita.

4. 医者：薬を出しますから、食事の後で、1錠（   ）飲んでください。
   Isha: Kusuri o dashimasu kara, shokuji no ato de, ichijō (   ) nonde kudasai.

5. 夫：ワインはあと何本（   ）残ってる？
   妻：そうね、まだ5本は残ってると思うわ。
   Otto: Wain wa ato nanbon (   ) nokotte 'ru?
   Tsuma: Sō ne, mada gohon wa nokotte 'ru to omou wa.

Answers and Translations for Quiz XII-2

1. とも (tomo). Fukui: You were taking two employment exams, right? How'd they go? Nakajima: As it turns out, I failed both.
2. くらい、ぐらい (kurai, gurai). Hotel guest: I'd like to order dinner through room service. About how long would that take? Hotel employee: It depends on what is ordered, but delivery can be made within (it shouldn't take more than) thirty minutes.
3. とも (tomo). Teacher: Today's test consists of two pages. Write on both pages in pencil. Students: Yes, Teacher.
4. ずつ (zutsu). Doctor: I'll prescribe some medicine for you. Take one pill each after meals.
5. ぐらい、くらい (gurai, kurai). Husband: About how many bottles of wine are left? Wife: Well, there are still five left over, I think.

XIII

The Particle の (No) Indicates that the Noun Preceding It Modifies the Noun Following It

1. の (no)

 の has no other particles in this book to which it can be profitably compared. But since it cannot be ignored entirely, I have chosen two common functions for inclusion. For other functions of の, see my *All About Particles*.

1. の (no). Indicates that the thing or person preceding の possesses, either literally or figuratively, the thing or person following the particle. Used with nouns. English equivalent: " 's," "of."

i) 私の傘はあそこにあります。
 Watashi **no** kasa wa asoko ni arimasu.
 My umbrella is over there.

ii) 会社の前にとまっているのは、社長の車です。
 Kaisha no mae ni tomatte iru no wa, shachō **no** kuruma desu.
 The car parked in front of the company is the President's.

 See also II-3, where の is used to specify locations.

2. の (no). Indicates that the thing or person preceding the particle belongs in some way to the group or organization that follows the particle. English equivalent: "of," "at."

i) あの大学の学生は、優秀な人が多いそうですね。
Ano daigaku **no** gakusei wa, yūshū na hito ga ōi sō desu ne.
There are a lot of excellent students at that university.

ii) これは私の会社の製品です。
Kore wa watashi **no** kaisha no seihin desu.
This is a product of my company.

QUIZ XIII

QUIZ XIII–1

This is essentially a quiz on の (no), but to make it more challenging, I have included a few other particles. Choose the correct ones from those given below the sample sentences. Answers and English translations follow the quiz.

1. 図書館（　　）中国語（　　）新聞（　　）あります。
   Toshokan (　) Chūgoku-go (　) shinbun (　) arimasu.

   1. の (no)　2. が (ga)　3. に (ni)

2. これ（　　）誰（　　）かばんですか？
   Kore (　) dare (　) kaban desu ka?

   1. の (no)　2. は (wa)

3. あなた（　　）学校は、東京（　　）何区（　　）あります か？
   Anata (　) gakkō wa, Tōkyō (　) nani-ku (　) arimasu ka?

   1. に (ni)　2. の (no)　3. で (de)

4. 川村さん（　　）家族（　　）今外国（　　）います。
   Kawamura-san (　) kazoku (　) ima gaikoku (　) imasu.

   1. は (wa)　2. に (ni)　3. の (no)

129

5. 私（　）家の近く（　　）、区（　　）公園があります。
   Watashi (　) ie (　) chikaku (　　), ku (　　) kōen ga arimasu.

   1. に (ni)   2. の (no)

Answers and Translations for Quiz XIII-1

1 = 2, 3, 1. The library has Chinese-language newspapers.
2 = 2, 1. Whose bag is this?
3 = 2, 2, 1. In which ward of Tokyo is your school?
4 = 3, 1, 2. Kawamura-san's family is now (living) overseas.
5 = 2, 1, 2. There is a public (ward) park near my house.

XIV

Sentence-ending Particles Indicating What the Speaker Has Heard

1. って (tte)
2. だと (da to)

✐ Both of these particles are commonly used in daily conversation among friends and family. A more formal way of saying the same thing is そうです (sō desu): e.g., 中田さんは来るそうです (Nakata-san wa kuru sō desu, "I hear that Nakata-san will come").

1. って (tte). Indicates what the speaker has heard from someone else and usually occurs in the form って (tte). It is typical of casual, everyday conversation among family and friends. In this sense, it can follow nouns (when って becomes だって [datte]), adjectives, and plain verb forms. When following verbs (e.g., 食べるって [taberu tte]), the form often becomes 食べるんだって (taberu n' datte). It has basically the same meaning as だと (da to; XIV-2), though the latter is somewhat more typical of men's speech and has a rougher tone. English equivalent: "I hear," "they say."

i) ゆみ：昨日の晩、真由から電話が来て、明日都合が悪くなって来られないんだって。
京子：本当？じゃ、私たちもやめようか。

Yumi: Kinō no ban, Mayu kara denwa ga kite, ashita tsugō ga waruku natte korarenai n' da**tte**.
Kyōko: Hontō? Ja, watashi-tachi mo yameyō ka.

Yumi: Last night I got a call from Mayu, and she says that something has come up and she can't come tomorrow.
Kyoko: Really? Well then, why don't we call it quits too?

ii) 義彦：今日の 経済原論のクラス、休講だって。
政夫：うそ、早起きして来たのに…

Yoshihiko: Kyō no keizai-genron no kurasu, kyūkō da**tte**.
Masao: Uso, hayaoki shite kita no ni …

Yoshihiko: Did you hear, today's class on economic principles has been cancelled.
Masao: You're kidding! And here I got up early just for that.

> ✐ A sentence ending with って can be made into a question by finishing the sentence with a slight rise in intonation (V-5). For a more polite effect, って can be used after verbs ending in ます (-masu) and after です (desu): 食べますって (tabemasu tte) and 食べるんですって (taberu n' desu tte).

2. だと (da to). Indicates what the speaker has heard from someone else. It is more typically used by men than women and is a rougher mode of speech than って (tte; XIV-1), and it is less commonly used. It can follow nouns directly, but when following verbs, ん (n) must intercede between verb and particle: e.g., 食べるんだと (taberu n' da to). English equivalent: "I hear," "they say."

i) 妹：お母さん、どうしてあわてて掃除なんかしてるの？
姉：今晩急にお客さんが来るん**だと**。

Imōto: Okāsan, dōshite awatete sōji nanka shite 'ru no?
Ane: Konban kyū ni okyaku-san ga kuru n' **da to**.

Younger sister: How come Mom is rushing around and cleaning up?
Older sister: She says that all of a sudden we're having guests tonight.

ii) 美加：毎日いい天気ね。
佳代：それが明日は雨**だと**。

Mika: Mainichi ii tenki ne.
Kayo: Sore ga ashita wa ame **da to**.

Mika: We're having good weather every day.
Kayo: But they say tomorrow is rain.

QUIZ XIV-1

Change the following sentences as shown in the example. Answers and English translations follow the quiz.

EXAMPLE
山本さんは来ると聞きました。
▶ 山本さん、来るって。
Yamamoto-san wa kuru to kikimashita.
▶ Yamamoto-san, kuru tte.

1. 明日、雨が降ると聞きました。
   ▶ _____
   Ashita, ame ga furu to kikimashita.
   ▶ _____

2. この映画は面白いと聞きました。
   ▶ _____
   Kono eiga wa omoshiroi to kikimashita.
   ▶ _____

3. 今桜がきれいだと聞きました。
   ▶ _____

Ima sakura ga kirei da to kikimashita.
▶ _____

4. 吉川さんは病気だと聞きました。
▶ _____
Yoshikawa-san wa byōki da to kikimashita.
▶ _____

5. あのレストランは安いと聞きました。
▶ _____
Ano resutoran wa yasui to kikimashita.
▶ _____

Answers and Translations for Quiz XIV-1

1. 明日、雨が降るって。
   Ashita, ame ga furu tte.
   I hear it's going to rain tomorrow.
2. この映画は面白いって。
   Kono eiga wa omoshiroi tte.
   They say this movie is interesting.
3. 今桜がきれいだって。
   Ima sakura ga kirei datte.
   They say the cherry blossoms are pretty now.
4. 吉川さんは病気だって。
   Yoshikawa-san wa byōki datte.
   I hear Yoshikawa-san is sick.
5. あのレストランは安いって。
   Ano resutoran wa yasui tte.
   They say that restaurant is cheap.

QUIZ XIV-2

Change the following sentences as shown in the example. Answers and English translations follow the quiz.

EXAMPLE
この映画はあまり面白くないそうです。
► この映画はあまり面白くないんだと。
Kono eiga wa amari omoshiroku nai sō desu.
► Kono eiga wa amari omoshiroku nai n' da to.

1. 今年の冬は寒いそうです。
   ►
   Kotoshi no fuyu wa samui sō desu.
   ►

2. ガソリンの値段が上がったそうです。
   ►
   Gasorin no nedan ga agatta sō desu.
   ►

3. 孝は明日の授業に来ないそうです。
   ►
   Takashi wa ashita no jugyō ni konai sō desu.
   ►

4. あの人は中国人だそうです。
   ►
   Ano hito wa Chūgoku-jin da sō desu.
   ►

5. 昨日の明け方，北海道で地震があったそうです。
   ▶
   Kinō no akegata, Hokkaidō de jishin ga atta sō desu.
   ▶

Answers and Translations for Quiz XIV-2

1. 今年の冬は寒いんだと。
   Kotoshi no fuyu wa samui n' da to.
   I hear that it's going to be cold this winter.
2. ガソリンの値段が上がったんだと。
   Gasorin no nedan ga agatta n' da to.
   I hear the price of gas has gone up.
3. 孝は明日の授業に来ないんだと。
   Takashi wa ashita no jugyō ni konai n' da to.
   I hear Takashi's not coming to tomorrow's class.
4. あの人は中国人だと。
   Ano hito wa Chūgoku-jin da to.
   I hear he is Chinese.
5. 昨日の明け方、北海道で地震があったんだと。
   Kinō no akegata, Hokkaidō de jishin ga atta n' da to.
   At dawn yesterday, there was an earthquake in Hokkaido, I hear.

XV

Particles that Indicate Emphasis

1. も (mo)
2. こそ (koso)
3. さえ (sae)
4. すら (sura)
5. ものなら (mono nara)
6. くせに (kuse ni)
7. どころか (dokoro ka)
8. ものを (mono o)
9. ぞ (zo)
10. ってば (tte ba)
11. ものか (mono ka)
12. ほど (hodo)

1. も (mo). Following nouns, indicates that an amount or quantity is large or more than expected. Often used for emphasis. English equivalent: "as much as," "as many as."

i) 昨日の晩、ビールを10本も飲んだので、今朝は二日酔いで頭が痛い。
Kinō no ban, bīru o juppon **mo** nonda no de, kesa wa futsuka-yoi de atama ga itai.
Last night I drank all of ten bottles of beer, and this morning I've got a headache from the hangover.

ii) 佐藤さんは、6か国語も話せるんだそうです。
Satō-san wa, rokkakoku-go **mo** hanaseru n' da sō desu.
Sato-san can speak as many as six languages, I hear.

⦿ As seen below, when も is used with the number one and a negative verb, it means "not even one."

i) 息子：暑いなあ、ジュースある？
母：冷蔵庫にあるでしょ。

息子：えっ、1本もないよ。

Musuko: Atsui nā, jūsu aru?
Haha: Reizōko ni aru desho.
Musuko: Ett, ippon **mo** nai yo.

Son: Gosh, it's hot. Is there any juice?
Mother: Right there in the frig.
Son: Hey, there's not a single bottle left.

ii) 教師：山下さん、教室に誰かいる？
山下：いいえ、もうみんな帰ってしまって、一人もいませんよ。

Kyōshi: Yamashita-san, kyōshitsu ni dare ka iru?
Yamashita: Iie, mō minna kaette shimatte, hitori **mo** imasen yo.

Teacher: Yamashita-san, is there anyone in the classroom?
Yamashita: No, they've all gone. Not a single person is left.

2. こそ (koso). Indicates that emphasis is to be placed on the word (the noun) preceding the particle. Most often occurs with positive verb forms. English equivalent: "for certain," "for sure."

i) 今年こそあの大学に合格したい。
Kotoshi **koso** ano daigaku ni gōkaku shitai.
This year for sure, I want to get accepted at that university.

ii) 山城：竹村さん、社長にならなかったそうですね。
林：そうなんですよ。竹村さんこそ次期社長だと思っていたんですけどね。

Yamashiro: Takemura-san, shachō ni naranakatta sō desu ne.
Hayashi: Sō nan desu yo. Takemura-san **koso** jiki-shachō da to omotte ita n' desu kedo ne.

Yamashiro: I understand that Takemura-san didn't become President.
Hayashi: That's right. I thought Takemura-san would definitely be the next president.

3. さえ (sae). Marks off something that, in context, is seen as occupying an extreme position, and in this sense means "even." When a clause ends in ば (-ba; VII-1) or たら (-tara; VII-2), the word preceding さえ shows what would be needed to satisfy the stated conditions, and means "if only." It is more widely used in casual everyday conversation than the more polite すら (sura; XV-4), with which it is interchangeable in the first function mentioned above. English equivalent: "even," "if only."

i) この質問は、子供で**さえ**すぐ答えられるほど、やさしいものです。
Kono shitsumon wa, kodomo de **sae** sugu kotaerareru hodo, yasashii mono desu.
This question is so easy that even a child could answer it.

ii) 山本さん**さえ**承知してくれれば、この仕事はうまくいくと思います。
Yamamoto-san **sae** shōchi shite kurereba, kono shigoto wa umaku iku to omoimasu.
If we can only get Yamamoto-san's approval, I think this job should proceed smoothly.

4. すら (sura). Marks off something that, in context, is seen as occupying an extreme position, and in this sense means "even." In contrast to さえ (sae; XV-3), すら is less used in casual daily conversation and does not follow ば (-ba; VII-1) or たら (-tara; VII-2). It is often followed by a negative verb. English equivalent: "even."

i) これは、学者で**すら**なかなか解けない難しい問題です。

Kore wa, gakusha de **sura** nakanaka tokenai muzukashii mondai desu.

This is a problem that even scholars have great difficulty in solving.

ii) あのオリンピック選手は事故にあって、歩くこと**すら**出来ない体になってしまったそうだ。

Ano orinpikku senshu wa jiko ni atte, aruku koto **sura** dekinai karada in natte shimatta sō da.

I heard that Olympic athlete met with an accident and ended up in such a condition that he can't even walk.

5. ものなら (mono nara). Places emphasis on the conditional nature of the clause that precedes it. It has two functions: 1) it indicates that if the conditional clause is carried out, the results are likely to be unfavorable; 2) it expresses a hope that the conditional clause will be fulfilled. ものなら is often replaceable by ば (-ba; VII-1) and たら (-tara; VII-2), but it is much more emphatic than either. It is preceded by a plain verb, a potential verb, or a verb in the -ō/-yō form. English equivalent: "if ... then."

i) 鈴木：社長は今日、機嫌が悪いようだね。
富田：そうなんですよ。何か言おう**ものなら**、怒鳴られそうですよ。

Suzuki: Shachō wa kyō, kigen ga warui yō da ne.
Tomita: Sō nan desu yo. Nani ka iō **mono nara**, donararesō desu yo.

Suzuki: Today the President seems to be in a bad mood.
Tomita: You're so right. If you try to say something, you feel you're going to get yelled at.

ii) 妻：もう一度、富士山に登りたいですね。
夫：登れる**ものなら**登りたいが、年を取って、体力が無くなったから、富士登山は無理だろう。

Tsuma: Mō ichido, Fuji-san ni noboritai desu ne.
Otto: Noboreru **mono nara** noboritai ga, toshi o totte, tairyoku ga nakunatta kara, Fuji-tozan wa muri darō.

Wife: I'd like to climb Mt. Fuji one more time.
Husband: If it was possible, I'd like to do it, but getting older and physically weaker, I'd say climbing Mt. Fuji is out of the question.

6. くせに (kuse ni). Indicates that judging from what precedes the particle, what follows is unexpected or unworthy and is deserving of censure. Often concerns someone who is trying to act beyond their ability or station in life. It is similar to のに (no ni), but much stronger in its sense of condemnation. English equivalent: "even though," "despite the fact that."

i) あの子は子供の**くせに**、毎晩ビールを飲んでいるそうだ。
Ano ko wa kodomo no **kuse ni**, maiban bīru o nonde iru sō da.
Despite the fact that she is still practically a child, I hear she drinks beer every night.

ii) あの人は、歌が下手な**くせに**、みんなの前で歌いたがるので困ります。
Ano hito wa, uta ga heta na **kuse ni**, minna no mae de utaitagaru no de komarimasu.
Even though he is really terrible at singing, it's a real problem because he's always wanting to sing in front of people.

7. どころか (dokoro ka). By denying what precedes it, どころか emphasizes what follows, which is quite the opposite of what might be expected. English equivalent: "far from," "more than."

i) 山岡：お子さん、夏休みにアメリカに行ってきて、英語話せるようになったんでしょう？
高田：とんでもない、英語**どころか**、日本人なのに漢字もろくに読めないんで困ってるのよ。

Yamaoka: Okosan, natsu-yasumi ni Amerika ni itte kite, eigo hanaseru yō ni natta n' deshō?
Takada: Tonde mo nai, eigo **dokoro ka**, Nihon-jin na no ni kanji mo roku ni yomenai n'de komatte 'ru no yo.

Yamaoka: Your children, they went to America during summer vacation, so they must be able to speak English now.
Takada: You must be kidding. Far from speaking English, they can't even read kanji properly, though they're Japanese. It's a problem.

ii) 光子：週末の登山、雨にあったんですって？
健二：雨**どころか**、雪まで降ってきて大変だったよ。

Mitsuko: Shūmatsu no tozan, ame ni atta n' desu tte?
Kenji: Ame **dokoro ka**, yuki made futte kite taihen datta yo.

Mitsuko: During your mountain climbing this week, I heard you ran into some rain?
Kenji: More than rain, it even started snowing and was pretty tough.

8. ものを (mono o). Indicates that if something had been done, then the unfavorable results that followed would not have occurred. English equivalent: "if only."

i) あの時黙っていればいい**ものを**、ついしゃべってしまった。
Ano toki damatte ireba ii **mono o**, tsui shabette shimatta.
If only I had kept quiet that time, but the words just slipped out.

ii) あんなに寒いときに、山登りになど行かなければいい**ものを**、あの人はでかけていった。
Anna ni samui toki ni, yamanobori ni nado ikanakereba ii **mono o**, ano hito wa dekakete itta.
As cold as it was then, he had no business going mountain climbing or anything like that, but he went anyway.

9. ぞ (zo). A sentence-ending particle that adds force to the entire sentence. Typical of men's speech, it is often used to warn of an impending danger or threat or as a verbal encouragement to oneself.

i) 雪が降ってきた**ぞ**。
Yuki ga futte kita **zo**.
Hey, it's started snowing.

ii) 津波が来る**ぞ**。
Tsunami ga kuru **zo**.
A tsunami is coming!

10. ってば (tteba). A sentence-ending particle that indicates the speaker's irritation that the listener has not understood or complied with what the speaker said. English equivalent: "I said," "Didn't I tell you."

i) わかった**ってば**。
Wakatta **tteba**.
I said I understood. / I understand, OK!

静かにして**ってば**。
Shizuka ni shite **tteba**.
Didn't I tell you to keep quiet. / Keep quiet, I say.

11. ものか (mono ka). A sentence-ending particle that negates the preceding verb and states the speaker's firm intention not to do something. It is typical of casual everyday conversation and has an even more casual form in もんか (mon ka). Both of these are more forceful than simply ending the sentence with a verb in the negative form. English equivalent: "I never want to ... again," "I'll never ... again."

i) もうあの店には二度と行く**ものか**。
Mō ano mise ni wa nido to iku **mono ka**.
I'll never go to that store again.

ii) あの人とはもう会う**ものか**。
Ano hito to wa mō au **mono ka**.
I never want to see him ever again.

iii) あいつには、もう会う**もんか**。
Aitsu ni wa, mō au **mon ka**.
I never want to lay eyes on that guy again.

12. ほど (hodo). Indicates the degree or extent to which an action is carried out, usually an extreme degree. English equivalent: "so ... that."

i) その日、私は死ぬ**ほど**疲れていた。
Sono hi, watashi wa shinu **hodo** tsukarete ita.
That day, I was so tired I thought I would die (I was dead tired).

ii) 電車は海水浴に行く人で、身動きできない**ほど**混んでいた。
Densha wa kaisuiyoku ni iku hito de, miugoki dekinai **hodo** konde ita.
The train was so full of people going to the beach to swim that you could hardly move an inch.

QUIZ XV

QUIZ XV-1

Choose the correct particle from those given below the sample sentences. Answers and English translations follow the quiz.

1. 山本さんは、来年(　　)ピアノのコンテストに入賞したいと、毎日8時間も練習をしている。
   Yamamoto-san wa, rainen (　　) piano no kontesuto ni nyūshō shitai to, mainichi hachijikan mo renshū o shite iru.

   1. くせに (kuse ni)　2. どころか (dokoro ka)　3. こそ (koso)　4. さえ (sae)

2. 野田：昨日林とけんかしたんだって？　あいつ悪かったって言ってたから、会ってやってくれよ。
   田川：いやだよ。あいつには、もう二度と会う(　　)。
   Noda: Kinō Hayashi to kenka shita n' datte? Aitsu warukatta tte itte 'ta kara, atte yatte kure yo.
   Tagawa: Iya da yo. Aitsu ni wa, mō nido to au (　　).

   1. どころか (dokoro ka)　2. ものか (mono ka)　3. ものなら (mono nara)　4. ものを (mono o)

3. 最近は仕事が忙しくて、旅行(　　)映画にも行けない。
   Saikin wa shigoto ga isogashikute, ryokō (　　) eiga ni mo ikenai.

   1. さえ (sae)　2. こそ (koso)　3. どころか (dokoro ka)　4. ものか (mono ka)

4. あの人は、そのことを知らない（　　　）、知っているような顔をしていた。
   Ano hito wa, sono koto o shiranai (　　), shitte iru yō na kao o shite ita.

   1. くせに (kuse ni)　2. こそ (koso)　3. どころか (dokoro ka)　4. ものか (mono ka)

5. 宏美：この映画、叔母様の若い頃とても人気があったそうですね。
   叔母：そうよ、私10回（　　　）観たわよ。
   Hiromi: Kono eiga, oba-sama no wakai koro totemo ninki ga atta sō desu ne.
   Oba: Sō yo, watashi jukkai (　　) mita wa yo.

   1. すら (sura)　2. も (mo)　3. さえ (sae)　4. こそ (koso)

6. 宏美：叔母様はヨーロッパに何度もいらしたんでしょう？
   叔母：行きましたよ。もし行ける（　　　）、もう一度パリに行きたいわ。
   Hiromi: Oba-sama wa Yōroppa ni nando mo irashita n' deshō?
   Oba: Ikimashita yo. Moshi ikeru (　　), mō ichido Pari ni ikitai wa.

   1. ものなら (mono nara)　2. ものか (mono ka)　3. どころか (dokoro ka)　4. ものを (mono o)

7. 直樹：昨日行ったバー、どうだった？
   武彦：だめ、だめ、サービスは悪いし、高いし、もう行く（　　　）って思った。
   Naoki: Kinō itta bā, dō datta?
   Takehiko: Dame, dame, sābisu wa warui shi, takai shi, mō iku (　　) tte omotta.

   1. どころか (dokoro ka)　2. ものを (mono o)　3. ものか (mono ka)　4. ものなら (mono nara)

148　QUIZ XV

8. あの山は、お年寄りで（　　）登れるほど、なだらかだそうです。

   Ano yama wa, otoshiyori de (　　) noboreru hodo, nadaraka da sō desu.

   1. さえ (sae)　2. ほど (hodo)　3. も (mo)　4. こそ (koso)

9. 長生きできる（　　）長生きして、この仕事を完成させたい。

   Nagaiki dekiru (　　) nagaiki shite, kono shigoto o kansei sasetai.

   1. ものを (mono o)　2. ものか (mono ka)　3. ものなら (mono nara)
   4. ほど (hodo)

10. 相談してくれれば、そのくらいのお金なら貸してあげた（　　）…

    Sōdan shite kurereba, sono kurai no okane nara kashite ageta (　　)…

    1. ものか (mono ka)　2. くせに (kuse ni)　3. ものなら (mono nara)
    4. ものを (mono o)

Answers and Translations for Quiz XV-1

1 = 3. Next year for certain, Yamamoto-san wants to win a prize in a piano competition, so she's practicing all of eight hours a day.

2 = 2. Noda: I hear you had a fight with Hayashi yesterday. He said that he was in the wrong, so you should see him. Tagawa: No way. I never want to see him again.

3 = 3. I'm so busy these days, I can't even see a movie, much less take a trip.

4 = 1. He doesn't know a thing about it, but he had this look on his face that said he knew everything.

5 = 2. Hiromi: This movie was quite popular when you were young, wasn't it, Auntie. Aunt: That's right. I saw it as many as ten times.

6 = 1. Hiromi: Auntie, you have been to Europe any number of times, right? Aunt: I sure have. And if I could go again, I'd like to go to Paris once more.

7 = 3. Naoki: How was the bar you went to yesterday? Takehiko: No good at all. The service is bad, and it's expensive. I'll never come here again, I thought.

8 = 1 or 3. That mountain is so gentle (has such gentle slopes) that even elderly people can climb it.

9 = 3. If I can possibly live a long life, I'd like to live one, so that I can complete this work.

10 = 4. If you had only discussed it with me, I could have lent you at least that much money.

XVI

Particles Used for Comparison

1. と (to)
2. より (yori)
3. ほど (hodo)
4. で (de)

1. と (to). Used to list two or more items when asking the listener to choose one of them. English equivalent: "or."

> 🖉 In giving an answer to a question in the と formula, the listener often places の方 (no hō; [the one] on this side) after his choice. の方 can be used regardless of the number of items involved, contrasting with より (yori; XVI-2), which is used only with two items.

i) 田中：りんご**と**みかん**と**どちらが好きですか？
   山岸：そうですね、甘ければみかん**の方**が好きですね。

   Tanaka: Ringo **to** mikan **to** dochira ga suki desu ka?
   Yamagishi: Sō desu ne, amakereba mikan **no hō** ga suki desu ne.

   Tanaka: Which do you like better, apples or mikan oranges?
   Yamagishi: Well, if they are sweet, I like mikan oranges better.

ii) 安田夫人：あの店**と**、この店**と**、どちらが安いんですか？

河田夫人：そうですね、野菜だったら、あの店**の方**が安いと思います。

Yasuda fujin: Ano mise **to**, kono mise **to**, dochira ga yasui n' desu ka?
Kawada fujin: Sō desu ne, yasai dattara, ano mise **no hō** ga yasui to omoimasu.

Mrs. Yasuda: Which is cheaper, this store or that store?
Mrs. Kawada: Well, as for vegetables, that store is cheaper, I think.

iii) 福田：紅茶と、コーヒーと日本茶の中で、どれが一番体にいいと思いますか？
山根：私は紅茶がいいと思いますが。

Fukuda: Kōcha **to**, kōhī **to** Nihon-cha no naka de, dore ga ichiban karada ni ii to omoimasu ka?
Yamane: Watashi wa kōcha ga ii to omoimasu ga.

Fukuda: Which do you think is best for your health—black tea, coffee, or Japanese tea?
Yamane: I personally think that black tea is best.

> ✐ In the above, note that when three or more items are compared, the last is frequently followed by の中で (no naka de; within), which makes use of the で discussed in XVI-4.

2. より (yori). Used when comparing two items. The item preceding the particle is the lesser of the two. Compare の方 (no hō; XVI-1, note), which can refer to more than two items. English equivalent: "more than."

i) タイは、沖縄の夏より暑い日が多いですよ。
Tai wa, Okinawa no natsu **yori** atsui hi ga ōi desu yo.
Thailand has many more hot days than Okinawa in summer.

ii) 徹：ヤンキースと、レッドソックスと、どっちが強いのかなあ。
貴之：今年はヤンキース**より**レッドソックスの方が強いらしいですよ。

Tōru: Yankīsu to, Reddosokkusu to, dotchi ga tsuyoi no ka nā.
Takayuki: Kotoshi wa Yankīsu **yori** Reddosokkusu no hō ga tsuyoi rashii desu yo.

Toru: I wonder which is stronger, the Yankees or the Red Socks.
Takayuki: This year the Red Socks seem to be stronger than the Yankees.

3. ほど (hodo). Used to indicate that one item is lesser in some way than another. The greater of the two is followed by ほど (in contrast to より [yori; XVI-2], which follows the lesser), and the following verb is in the negative. ほど often follows nouns, but it can also follow verbs. English equivalent: "not as ... as."

i) 富士山は日本では高い山ですが、エベレスト**ほど**ではありません。
Fuji-san wa Nihon de wa takai yama desu ga, Eberesuto **hodo** de wa arimasen.
In Japan, Mt. Fuji is a tall mountain, but it is not as tall as Mt. Everest.

ii) 康子：英子、この頃ピアノうまくなったわね。
英子：ありがとう。でもまだ先生**ほど**上手に弾けないわ。

Yasuko: Eiko, kono goro piano umaku natta wa ne.
Eiko: Arigatō. Demo mada sensei **hodo** jōzu ni hikenai wa.

Yasuko: Eiko, your piano has really improved these days.
Eiko: Thanks. But I still can't play as well as my teacher.

4. で (de) Indicates the area or category in which three or more items are compared to find which is superior. Compare this to と (to; XVI-1), which states explicitly what the items for comparison are. English equivalent: "in," "throughout."

    i) あれは今東京で、一番高い建物です。
       Are wa ima Tōkyō **de**, ichiban takai tatemono desu.
       Right now that is the tallest building in Tokyo.

    ii) 世界で一番人口の多い国は、どこだと思いますか？
       Sekai **de** ichiban jinkō no ōi kuni wa, doko da to omoimasu ka?
       What country in the world do you think has the largest population?

QUIZ XVI

QUIZ XVI–1

Choose the correct particle from those given below the sample sentences. Answers and translations follow the quiz.

1. サンズの中(　　)、一番小さい選手は誰でしょうか？
   Sanzu no naka (　　), ichiban chiisai senshu wa dare deshō ka?

   1. と (to)   2. で (de)   3. も (mo)   4. を (o)

2. 美香：あの白いバッグ(　　)この黒いバッグと、どちらがすきですか？
   Mika: Ano shiroi baggu (　　) kono kuroi baggu to, dochira ga suki desu ka?

   1. も (mo)   2. が (ga)   3. で (de)   4. と (to)

   陽子：黒いバッグ(　　)方がすきです。
   Yōko: Kuroi baggu (　　) hō ga suki desu.

   1. と (to)   2. の (no)   3. より (yori)   4. で (de)

3. 今年の夏は、去年の夏(　　)暑い。
   Kotoshi no natsu wa, kyonen no natsu (　　) atsui.

   1. の (no)   2. より (yori)   3. と (to)   4. も (mo)

4. 弘子は睦子（　　）背が高くない。
   Hiroko wa Mutsuko (　) se ga takaku nai.
   1. より (yori)　2. の (no)　3. で (de)　4. ほど (hodo)

5. 私はピアノ曲はバイオリンの曲（　　）好きではありません。
   Watashi wa piano-kyoku wa baiorin no kyoku (　) suki de wa arimasen.
   1. ほど (hodo)　2. まで (made)　3. の (no)　4. と (to)

Answers and Translations for Quiz XVI-1

1 = 2. Who is the shortest player on the Suns?
2 = 4, 2. Mika: Which do you like better, that white bag or this black one? Yoko: I prefer the black bag.
3 = 2. Summer this year is hotter than last summer.
4 = 4. Hiroko is not as tall as Mutsuko.
5 = 1. I don't like piano music as much as I like violin music.

XVII

Particles that Indicate a Means by which Something Is Done or Material from which Something Is Made

1. で (de)
2. で、から (de, kara)

1. で (de). Indicates a means or way of doing something. English equivalent: "by," "with."

i) 山本：会社まで、車で通っていますか？
河田：いいえ、この頃は電車で通ってます。

Yamamoto: Kaisha made, kuruma **de** kayotte imasu ka?
Kawada: Iie, kono goro wa densha **de** kayotte 'masu.

Yamamoto: Are you commuting to work by car?
Kawada: No, recently I've been commuting by train.

ii) この書類は、ボールペンで書いてください。
Kono shorui wa, bōrupen **de** kaite kudasai.
Please fill out these forms with a ball-point pen.

iii) 日本人は箸で食べることが多い。
Nihon-jin wa hashi **de** taberu koto ga ōi.
Japanese generally eat with chopsticks.

2. で、から (de, kara). Indicates the material with which, or from which, something is made. English equivalent: "from," "out of."

> ✐ Both of these particles can be equally used to indicate material, but when the nature of the material is obvious to the naked eye, such as with wood, paper, leather, cloth, and glass, the preference is for で to be used.

i) 豆腐は大豆から／で作ります。
Tōfu wa daizu **kara/de** tsukurimasu.
Tofu is made of soybeans.

ii) チョコレートは、カカオとミルクと砂糖で／から作ります。
Chokorēto wa, kakao to miruku to satō **de/kara** tsukurimasu.
Chocolate is made of cacao, milk, and sugar.

QUIZ XVII

QUIZ XVII–1

Choose the correct particle from those listed below the sample sentences. Answers and translations follow the quiz.

1. ジム：日本酒、おいしいですね。
   橋本：酒は米（　　　）作るんですよ。
   Jimu: Nihon-shu, oishii desu ne.
   Hashimoto: Sake wa kome (　　) tsukuru n' desu yo.

   1. から (kara)　2. と (to)　3. を (o)　4. も (mo)

2. パソコン（　　　）メールを送ります。
   Pasokon (　　) mēru o okurimasu.

   1. と (to)　2. も (mo)　3. で (de)　4. を (o)

3. 木（　　）作った家具は、暖かみがあります。
   Ki (　　) tsukutta kagu wa, atatakami ga arimasu.

   1. が (ga)　2. から (kara)　3. で (de)　4. も (mo)

4. 洋子：このケーキ、すごくおいしいわ。
   民子：ありがとう。お米の粉と砂糖（　　　）作ったの。
   Yōko: Kono kēki, sugoku oishii wa.
   Tamiko: Arigatō. Okome no kona to satō (　　) tsukutta no.

   1. や (ya)　2. で (de)　3. など (nado)　4. と (to)

159

5. 川口：アフリカのそんな奥地までどうやって行ったの？
　　花森：バイク（　　）行ったんだ。
   Kawaguchi: Afurika no sonna okuchi made dō yatte itta no?
   Hanamori: Baiku (　　) itta n' da.

   1. と (to)　　2. も (mo)　　3. で (de)　　4. から (kara)

Answers and Translations for Quiz XVII-1

1 = 1. Jim: Japanese sake is really good. Hashimoto: It's made from rice, you know.
2 = 3. Email is sent with a PC. / I'll send an email with my PC.
3 = 3. Furniture made of wood has a certain warmth.
4 = 2. Yoko: This cake is totally delicious. Tamiko: Thanks. I made it with rice powder and sugar.
5 = 3. Kawaguchi: How did you ever get that far into the interior of Africa? Hanamori: I went by motorcycle.

XVIII

Particles that Indicate a Purpose or Object of a Verb

1. に (ni)
2. を (o)

1. に (ni). Indicates the purpose or goal of an action. It follows the ます (-masu) stem of a verb and is followed in turn by another verb: e.g., 食べに行く (tabe **ni** iku), "to go to eat." English equivalent: "to."

i) レストランへイタリア料理を食べに行きます。
Resutoran e Itaria ryōri o tabe **ni** ikimasu.
We are going to a restaurant to eat Italian food.

ii) 午後から図書館へ本を借りに行きます。
Gogo kara toshokan e hon o kari **ni** ikimasu.
First thing this afternoon I am going to the library to borrow a book.

iii) この頃、映画を見に行く時間がありません。
Kono goro, eiga o mi **ni** iku jikan ga arimasen.
These days I don't have time to go and see a movie.

2. を (o). Indicates the immediate object of an action: i.e., the direct object of a transitive verb. In イタリア料理を食べる (Itaria ryōri **o**

taberu), イタリア料理 is the direct object of 食べる. Combining this with に (ni; XVIII-1, indicating purpose) results in the following: イタリア料理**を**食べ**に**行く (Itaria ryōri **o** tabe **ni** iku).

   i) 日本料理の作り方**を**習いたいんです。
      Nihon ryōri no tsukurikata **o** naraitai n' desu.
      I want to learn how to cook Japanese food.

   ii) 毎朝新聞**を**読みます。
      Maiasa shinbun **o** yomimasu.
      I read the newspaper every morning.

   iii) 今月は、新しい洋服**を**買うつもりです。
      Kongetsu wa, atarashii yōfuku **o** kau tsumori desu.
      I plan on buying some new clothes this month.

   iv) 夜は友達にメール**を**送ります。
      Yoru wa tomodachi ni mēru **o** okurimasu.
      I send email to friends at night.

QUIZ XVIII

QUIZ XVIII–1

Choose the direct particle from those given directly below to insert into the parentheses in the sample sentences. Answers and English translations follow the quiz.

Place the correct particle in the parentheses:
に (ni)　か (ka)　を (o)

1. 由里：喉が渇いたわ。
   豊：僕も。コーヒーでも飲み（　　）行こう。
   Yuri: Nodo ga kawaita wa.
   Yutaka: Boku mo. Kōhī de mo nomi (　　) ikō.

2. 日曜日、美術館へ展覧会（　　）見（　　）行ってきました。
   Nichiyōbi, bijutsukan e tenrankai (　　) mi (　　) itte kimashita.

3. 咲恵：図書館へ行くの？
   明：そう、法学の参考書（　　）探し（　　）行くんだ。
   Sakie: Toshokan e iku no?
   Akira: Sō, hōgaku no sankōsho (　　) sagashi (　　) iku n' da.

4. 夕べは、ピアノのコンサート（　　）聞き（　　）行きました。
   Yūbe wa, piano no konsāto (　　) kiki (　　) ikimashita.

5. 今運転（　　）習っていますが、難しいです。
   Ima unten (　　) naratte imasu ga, muzukashii desu.

163

Answers and Translations for Quiz XVIII-1

1. に (ni). Yuri: I'm thirsty. Yutaka: Me too. Let's go have some coffee.
2. を (o), に (ni). On Sunday I went to an art gallery to see an exhibition.
3. を (o), に (ni). Sakie: Going to the library? Akira: Yeah, I'm going to look for a legal reference book.
4. を (o), に (ni). Yesterday evening I went to hear a piano concert.
5. を (o). Right now I'm learning to drive, but it's hard.

QUIZ XVIII–2

Change the conjugation of the verb in parentheses, as in the example. Answers and English translations follow the quiz.

EXAMPLE
プールに(泳ぐ)に行きます。 ►泳ぎ
Pūru ni (oyogu) ni ikimasu. ►oyogi

1. 郵便局へ小包を(出す)に行きます。 ►_____
   Yūbinkyoku e kozutsumi o (dasu) ni ikimasu. ►_____

2. 家へ食事を(する)に帰ります。 ►_____
   Ie e shokuji o (suru) ni kaerimasu. ►_____

3. デパートへ靴を(買う)に行ってきます。 ►_____
   Depāto e kutsu o (kau) ni itte kimasu. ►_____

4. 研究室へ先生に(会う)に行きました。 ►_____
   Kenkyūshitsu e sensei ni (au) ni ikimashita. ►_____

5. 船で沖へイルカを(見る)に行けますよ。 ►_____
   Fune de oki e iruka o (miru) ni ikemasu yo. ►_____

Answers and Translations for XVIII-2

1. 出し (dashi). I'm going to the post office to send out a package.
2. し (shi). I'm going home to eat.
3. 買い (kai). I'm going out to the department store to buy some shoes.
4. 会い (ai). I went to his office/lab to see the teacher/professor.
5. 見 (mi). You can go offshore by boat to see the dolphins.

XIX

Particles that Come at the End of a Sentence and Indicate the Speaker's Feelings or Dictate the Tone of a Sentence

1. か (ka)
2. さ (sa)
3. じゃん (jan)
4. けど (kedo)
5. な、なあ (na, nā)
6. もの (mono)
7. の (no)
8. ね (ne)
9. や (ya)
10. よ (yo)
11. わ (wa)
12. やら (yara)
13. が (ga)
14. から、ので (kara, no de)

1. か (ka). Indicates a rhetorical question made by the speaker when talking to himself or herself. The question generally concerns the discovery of new information about something which the speaker has known about before. Typical of casual everyday conversation among family and friends. English equivalent: "so ..."

i) あの人もとうとう亡くなった**か**。
Ano hito mo tōtō nakunatta **ka**.
So now he has also passed away.

ii) 義彦も、やっとあの大学に合格できた**か**。
Yoshihiko mo, yatto ano daigaku ni gōkaku dekita **ka**.
So Yoshihiko has also finally managed to get accepted at that university.

2. さ (sa). Indicates that what precedes the particle is not to be taken seriously, is something obvious, or is a matter of course. It is typical of casual everyday, masculine conversation among friends and family. さ

contrasts with よ (yo; XIX-10), where the urge to press one's message on the other party is much stronger.

   i) 高松：山本、あの会社首になったんだってね。
      鈴木：あんなに休んでばっかりいたんだから、仕方がないさ。

    Takamatsu: Yamamoto, ano kaisha kubi ni natta n' datte ne.
    Suzuki: Anna ni yasunde bakkari ita n' da kara, shikata ga nai **sa**.

    Takamatsu: Did you hear Yamamoto got fired from that company?
    Suzuki: He was always taking off so often. It really can't be helped.

   ii) 佐和子：昨日のテニスの試合、勝ったの？
      孝：もちろん勝ったさ。相手はテニス始めたばっかりの奴だったから。

    Sawako: Kinō no tenisu no shiai, katta no?
    Takashi: Mochiron katta **sa**. Aite wa tenisu hajimeta bakkari no yatsu datta kara.

    Sawako: Did you win the tennis match yesterday?
    Takashi: Of course I won. The other guy had just started playing tennis.

3. じゃん (jan). Used as at the end of sentences by young Japanese to confirm what the listener knows, sometimes with an element of criticism. It is an truncated version of じゃない (ja nai; isn't it).

   i) 靖：昨日の晩、約束したのに飲み会に来なかった**じゃん**。
      忠夫：ごめん、バイトが終わらなくて行けなかった。

    Yasushi: Kinō no ban, yakusoku shita no ni nomikai ni konakatta **jan**.
    Tadao: Gomen, baito ga owaranakute ikenakatta.

Yasushi: Even though you'd promised, you didn't show up at the drinking party last night.
Tadao: Sorry. My temp job just never ended and I couldn't make it.

ii) 香：由香はあの映画すごく面白かったって言ってた**じゃん**。でもぜんぜん 面白くなかった。
由香：本当？ 私は面白かったのに。

Kaori: Yuka wa ano eiga sugoku omoshirokatta tte itte 'ta **jan**. Demo zenzen omoshiroku nakatta.
Yuka: Hontō? Watashi wa omoshirokatta no ni.

Kaori: Yuka said the movie was totally interesting, right, but it wasn't interesting at all.
Yuka: Really? But it was interesting to me.

4. けど (kedo). Coming at the end of a sentence or utterance, けど (literally, but) seems to show hesitation on the speaker's part by ending the sentence with "but" and leaving the rest unspoken. This show of hesitation is made for the sake of politeness (by leaving a direct expression of one's thoughts unspoken), but the meaning is generally clear. けど is often used as an indirect way of expressing an opposing opinion. It is similar to が (ga; XIX-13) in leaving the end of the sentence unspoken.

i) 部長：コピー、1部足りないよ。
秘書：そうですか？ 10部コピーしたつもりだったんで**すけど**…

Buchō: Kopī, ichibu tarinai yo.
Hisho: Sō desu ka? Jūbu kopī shita tsumori datta n' desu **kedo**…

Department head: We're one copy short.
Secretary: Is that so? But I thought that I had made ten copies.

ii) 貴之：まだ来ない人が4人いるよ。ちゃんと来るかな。
弘子：昨日の晩、みんなにメールしておいたんです**けど**…

Takayuki: Mada konai hito ga yonin iru yo. Chanto kuru ka na.
Hiroko: Kinō no ban, minna ni mēru shite oita n' desu **kedo** ...

Takayuki: Four people still haven't come. I wonder if they'll make it alright.
Hiroko: Last night I did send out an email to everyone, though.

5. な、なあ (na, nā). Used by men to soften the expression of an emotion, desire, judgment, or assertion. It is typical of casual everyday conversation among family and friends but inappropriate when speaking to superiors or in polite conversation with strangers. な、なあ contrasts with よ (yo; XIX-10), which is more assertive in making a statement.

i) 松田：岸田君、先月、子供が生まれたんだって？
山本：へえ、それは知らなかった**なあ**。

Matsuda: Kishida-kun, sengetsu, kodomo ga umareta n' datte?
Yamamoto: Hē, sore wa shiranakatta **nā**.

Matsuda: Did you hear that Kishida had a baby last month?
Yamamoto: Really! I didn't know that.

ii) 阿部：営業の武田君、北海道へ転勤だって？
本村：そうらしい**なあ**、子供が学校だから、大変だ**なあ**。

Abe: Eigyō no Takeda-kun, Hokkaidō e tenkin datte?
Motomura: Sō rashii **nā**, kodomo ga gakkō da kara, taihen da **nā**.

Abe: Did you hear that Takeda in Sales is being transferred to Hokkaido?
Motomura: It seems that way. His child's still in school [and may therefore have to transfer to Hokkaido, make new friends, etc.], so it's pretty tough.

6. もの (mono). Indicates a reason for something that is also a justification for the speaker's behavior. It is different from から、ので (kara, no de; XIX-14) in being much softer and feminine, much less direct, and much more of an appeal for leniency or indulgence. It is used principally by women, but in its casual form, もん (mon), it is used by both men and women of all ages.

i) 礼子：どうして、こんなに遅く来たの？
　　昌子：今朝は疲れていて、早く起きられなかったんですもの。

Reiko: Dōshite, konna ni osoku kita no?
Masako: Kesa wa tsukarete ite, hayaku okirarenakatta n' desu **mono**.

Reiko: How come you've gotten here so late?
Masako: I was so tired this morning, I couldn't get up early. You know how it is.

ii) 昭彦：昨日の練習試合に来なかったね。
　　久子：私、試合のこと、全然知らなかったんですもの。

Akihiko: Kinō no renshū-jiai ni konakatta ne.
Hisako: Watashi, shiai no koto, zenzen shiranakatta n' desu **mono**.

Akihiko: You didn't show up at the practice game yesterday.
Hisako: Practice game, I didn't hear a word about any practice game.

7. の (no). Indicates the softening of a statement with a falling intonation (a question with a rising intonation). Used principally by women.

i) 美子：明日何か予定ある？
　　宏美：この2、3日、頭が痛いから、病院へ行こうと思ってるの。

Yoshiko: Ashita nanika yotei aru?
Hiromi: Kono ni-san-nichi, atama ga itai kara, byōin e ikō to omotte 'ru **no**.

Yoshiko: Do you have anything planned for tomorrow?
Hiromi: These last two or three days I've had a headache, so I am thinking of going to the hospital.

ii) 由美：昨日のデート、楽しかった？
久子：それが、彼、来られなかったの。

Yumi: Kinō no dēto, tanoshikatta?
Hisako: Sore ga, kare, korarenakatta no.

Yumi: Have fun on your date yesterday?
Hisako: Actually, he couldn't come.

8. ね (ne). Seeks agreement or approval from the listener. Used by both men and women in all situations. よね (yo ne; mostly masculine) and わね (wa ne; mostly feminine) have the same basic meaning but are more forceful.

i) 東山：山本君もこの意見には同意してくれましたよね。
山本：もちろん同意しましたよ。

Higashiyama: Yamamoto-kun mo kono iken ni wa dōi shite kuremashita yo **ne**.
Yamamoto: Mochiron dōi shimashita yo.

Higashiyama: Yamamoto, you agreed with this view of the matter, am I right?
Yamamoto: I did agree, of course.

ii) 娘：ねえ、スカート、買ってもらっていいわね。
母：いいわ、でも1枚だけよ。

Musume: Nē, sukāto, katte moratte ii wa **ne**.
Haha: Ii wa, demo ichimai dake yo.

Daughter: You're going to buy me this skirt, aren't you.
Mother: Alright, but just that one.

9. や (ya). A casual masculine form used when talking to oneself and trying to convince oneself of something. It is similar to な、なあ (na, nā; XIX-5) in this respect, though や is more abrupt and has less heart-felt feeling.

i) 今日の試験はできなかったなあ。勉強してなかったんだから、仕方がない**や**。
Kyō no shiken wa dekinakatta nā. Benkyō shite 'nakatta n' da kara, shikata ga nai **ya**.
I didn't do so well on today's test. But I didn't study for it either, so what are you going to do.

ii) 朝から雨か。今日はテニスには行けない**や**。
Asa kara ame ka. Kyō wa tenisu ni wa ikenai **ya**.
Rain from morning on. I won't be able to go and play tennis today, will I.

10. よ (yo). Indicates an attempt to obtain the listener's approval or agreement by forcefully presenting one's opinion. Used by both men and women. Masculine usage often appears as だよ (da yo) and women's as either のよ (no yo) or わよ (wa yo).

i) 大塚：木村君がまず部長に相談すればよかったんだ**よ**。
長田：そうなんだ**よ**。

Ōtsuka: Kimura-kun ga mazu buchō ni sōdan sureba yokatta n' da **yo**.
Nagata: Sō nan da **yo**.

Otsuka: Kimura should have first talked to the department head, that's what.
Nagata: You're absolutely right.

ii) 知香：昨日どうして来なかったの**よ**？
信子：行ったの**よ**。でも時間間違えていったから、もう誰もいなかったの。

Chika: Kinō dōshite konakatta no **yo**?
Nobuko: Itta no **yo**. Demo jikan machigaete itta kara, mō dare mo inakatta no.

Chika: How come you didn't show up yesterday?
Nobuko: I did show up. But I went at the wrong time, so nobody was there.

11. わ (wa). Used by women to soften expressions of determination, desire, intent, and emotion. For わ in combination with ね (ne), see XIX-8, and with よ (yo), see XIX-10.

i) 母：ちょっと買い物に行ってくる**わ**。留守番お願いね。
娘：いい**わ**よ。

Haha: Chotto kaimono ni itte kuru **wa**. Rusuban onegai ne.
Musume: Ii **wa** yo.

Mother: I'm going out for a little shopping. Look after things, alright?
Daughter: No problem at all.

ii) 元子：明日映画に行かない？
章子：明日は無理だ**わ**。あさって試験があるから。

Motoko: Ashita eiga ni ikanai?
Akiko: Ashita wa muri da **wa**. Asatte shiken ga aru kara.

Motoko: Want to go to a movie tomorrow?
Akiko: Tomorrow's impossible for me. I've got a test the day after that.

12. やら (yara). Indicates strong doubts about issues of who, when, where, how, etc., concerning the matter in question. An interrogative word usually appears early in the sentence or immediately before やら. The particle itself often follows の (no).

> i) 祖父：太郎は勉強しているの？
> 　　祖母：コンピュータゲームばかりしてるわ。
> 　　祖父：いつ勉強するの**やら**…
>
> Sofu: Tarō wa benkyō shite iru no?
> Sobo: Konpyūta-gēmu bakari shite 'ru wa.
> Sofu: Itsu benkyō suru no **yara** …
>
> Grandfather: Is Taro studying?
> Grandmother: He's doing nothing but play computer games.
> Grandfather: Who knows when he studies.
>
> ii) 毎日暑くて、いつになったら涼しくなるの**やら**…
> Mainichi atsukute, itsu ni nattara suzushiku naru no **yara** …
> It's so hot every day, who knows when it will get cooler.

13. が (ga). Follows an expression of hope that something will turn out well but leaves open the possibility of an unfavorable outcome. が may be thought of as meaning "but." It is quite similar to けど (kedo; XIX-4), though somewhat more muffled in impact.

> i) 竹内：部長のお子さん、交通事故に遭われたそうですね。
> 　　山本：そうだそうですね。たいしたことないと、いいんです**が**…
>
> Takeuchi: Buchō no okosan, kōtsū-jiko ni awareta sō desu ne.
> Yamamoto: Sō da sō desu ne. Taishita koto nai to, ii n' desu **ga** ….

Takeuchi: I heard the department head's child met with a traffic accident.
Yamamoto: That's what they say. I hope it is nothing serious.

ii) 台風が来るそうだが、被害がないといい**が**…
Taifū ga kuru sō da ga, higai ga nai to ii **ga** …
A typhoon is said to be coming. I hope there is no damage from it.

14. から、ので (kara, no de). Indicates a reason for not doing something but does not say explicitly that it cannot be done. This is often used as a polite means of turning down requests, by giving a reason why the request must be turned down but avoiding actually turning it down in so many words.

i) 妻：そんなに毎日たばこをすっていたら、体をこわすわよ。
夫：来週やめる**から**…

Tsuma: Sonna ni mainichi tabako o sutte itara, karada o kowasu wa yo.
Otto: Raishū yameru **kara** …

Wife: If you smoke every day like that, you're going to ruin your health.
Husband: Well, I'm quitting next week.

ii) 前田：来週の土曜日、映画を見に行きませんか？
谷口：すみません。土曜日は先約があります**ので**…

Maeda: Raishū no doyōbi, eiga o mi ni ikimasen ka?
Taniguchi: Sumimasen. Doyōbi wa sen'yaku ga arimasu **no de** …

Maeda: Would you like to go see a movie next Saturday?
Taniguchi: I'm sorry, but I have a previous engagement on Saturday.